YOUTH, CRITICAL LITERACIES, AND CIVIC ENGAGEMENT

Through stories of youth using their many voices in and out of school—performance and parody, cartoons and poetry—to explore and express their ideas about the world, this book brings to the forefront the reality of lived literacy experiences of adolescents in today's urban culture in which literacy practices reflect important cultural messages about the interplay of local and global civic engagement. The focus is on three areas of youth civic engagement and cultural critique: homelessness, violence, and performing adolescence.

The authors explore how youth appropriate the arts, media, and literacy as resources and how this enables them to express their identities and engage in social and cultural engagement and critique. The book describes how the youth in the various projects represented entered the public sphere; the claims they made; the ways readers might think about pedagogical engagements, practice, and goals as forms of civic engagement; and implications for critical and arts and media-based literacy pedagogies in schools. It calls for more uncommon curricula that address the energies, skills, and resources that young people bring to the classroom and that forward democratic citizenship in a time when we are losing sight of issues of equity and social justice in our communities and nations.

Theresa Rogers is Professor, Language & Literacy Education, University of British Columbia, Canada.

Kari-Lynn Winters is Associate Professor of Drama Education, Brock University, Canada.

Mia Perry is Director of Research at the ecl foundation and based in Scotland, UK.

Anne-Marie LaMonde is Instructor, Teacher Education, University of British Columbia, Canada.

YOUTH, CRITICAL LITERACIES, AND CIVIC ENGAGEMENT

Arts, Media, and Literacy in the Lives of Adolescents

Theresa Rogers
Kari-Lynn Winters, Mia Perry,
and Anne-Marie LaMonde

Routledge
Taylor & Francis Group

NEW YORK AND LONDON

First published 2015
by Routledge
711 Third Avenue, New York, NY 10017

and by Routledge
2 Park Square, Milton Park, Abingdon, Oxon OX14 4RN

Routledge is an imprint of the Taylor & Francis Group, an informa business

© 2015 Taylor & Francis

The right of the author to be identified as author of this work has been asserted by him/her in accordance with sections 77 and 78 of the Copyright, Designs and Patents Act 1988.

Trademark notice: Product or corporate names may be trademarks or registered trademarks, and are used only for identification and explanation without intent to infringe.

Library of Congress Cataloging-in-Publication Data
Rogers, Theresa.
    Youth, critical literacies, and civic engagement : arts, media, and literacy in the lives of adolescents / by Theresa Rogers, Kari-Lynn Winters, Mia Perry, and Anne-Marie LaMonde.
        pages cm
    Includes bibliographical references and index.
    1. Education, Urban—British Columbia—Vancouver.   2. Arts—Study and teaching (Secondary)—British Columbia—Vancouver.   3. Urban poor—British Columbia—Vancouver—Education.   4. Youth with social disabilities—British Columbia—Vancouver—Education.   I. Winters, Kari-Lynn, 1969-   II. Perry, Mia.   III. LaMonde, Anne-Marie.   IV. Title.
    LC5125.R64 2014
    370.9173'2097112—dc23
    2014026112

ISBN: 978-1-138-01744-3 (hbk)
ISBN: 978-1-138-01745-0 (pbk)
ISBN: 978-1-315-78048-1 (ebk)

Typeset in Bembo
by Apex CoVantage, LLC

CONTENTS

FOREWORD

Youth literacies are never more visible than when they occur outside the proverbial classroom door. Walk down any locker-filled hallway in high schools across much of North America at dismissal time and you'll see young people opening their mobile devices before unlocking their lockers. They're reading and texting as if there were no tomorrow. Why? Communicating with the outside world is not something they like to put on hold for too long at a time; nor are they at a loss for the literate practices needed to participate in today's mobile technology.

Yet this scenario fails to tell the whole story. In fact, it pales in comparison with the art- and media-infused youth literacies that Theresa Rogers and her colleagues, Kari-Lynn Winters, Mia Perry, and Anne-Marie LaMonde, chronicle in this relatively brief but compelling book. *Youth, Critical Literacies, and Civic Engagement* documents systematically how adolescents and young adults combine written texts with the visual and performing arts to substantiate their claim of civic-mindedness in contemporary urban settings. Rogers, working with others, captures the remarkable talent of these young people through research made accessible by a writing style that she has honed to perfection over the years. The result is a book that educators, parents, and local civic leaders will find worthwhile and memorable if for no other reason than it makes them smarter and better grounded in the contributions youth can, and do, make in the communities of which they are a part.

What intrigues me most about the YouthCLAIM project—the focal point of Rogers and her co-authors' work—is its insistence on an integrative look at three separate programs: one for homeless youth, another on community anti-violence, and yet another on a unique secondary school drama program. Though distinct cultural entities and separated by geographic locales within a large world city, the three represent the strengths and challenges brought about by universal and fast-paced changes in education. Readers fortunate enough to take the time to acquaint themselves with issues common to *Youth, Critical Literacies, and Civic Engagement* will find new meaning in what has traditionally been labeled citizenship. And with that new meaning in mind comes an enhanced appreciation for why this book is where we're at, globally and locally.

Donna Alvermann
The University of Georgia

PREFACE

As a team of educators who participate in the arts through writing, visual arts, video production, and theatre, we were interested in the intersections of arts, media, and critical literacy in the lives of youth in and out of schools as expressions of how they experienced their lives and social worlds; that is, we wanted to hear their claims about contemporary cultural issues and what alternatives they imagined for themselves and others.

We began the multi-year YouthCLAIM project from which this book grows in 2007, with funding from the Canadian government. At that time Vancouver was emerging as a North American global city and was on the verge of hosting the 2010 Olympics, an event that provoked public dialogues about the city itself as a player on the world stage. The city was rife with debates about the cost of the games in relation to much-needed social services, the contrasting images of a city of wealth and poverty, and the policies that were being enacted to present a more sanitized view of the city. The youth, as cultural critics, questioned these developments and policies and other urban issues related to homelessness, violence, and contemporary adolescence, actively engaging in public dialogue through their work.

We thoroughly enjoyed working with the youth in two community sites and one school site and experiencing their energy, talents, and perspectives on the city and the world across several years of the project. Over time we realized that this project was not only about youth arts, media, and literacy practices, but also about youth civic engagement, and ultimately points to the tensions between the literacy practices in schools and the kinds of active and engaged youth participation in public life.

Overview of the Book

Chapter 1 provides the context and the theoretical and methodological framing for the book. Chapters 2, 3, and 4 reflect the themes of student productions at each site—homelessness, violence, and performing contemporary adolescence—to illustrate how the youth used arts, media, and literacy as creative tools of expression and critique, addressing local and wider audiences to make claims about their lives and the world they find themselves in. Chapter 5, the closing chapter, further theorizes youth engagement in public pedagogy in relation to current conversations about youth, literacies, and local/global contexts and discourses. We describe how the youth in the various projects entered the public sphere, the claims they made, and the ways we might think about pedagogical engagements, practices, and goals as forms of civic engagement. We close with implications for critical arts and media-based literacy pedagogies in schools. We call for more uncommon curricula that address the energies, skills, and resources that young people bring to the classroom and that forward democratic citizenship in a time when we are losing sight of issues of equity and social justice in our communities and nations.

Acknowledgments

We would like to acknowledge the mentors, staff, and youth we worked with in these three sites. All were committed to their programs and generously gave us the opportunity to collaborate with them over the course of a year or more that we worked with them at each site.

Theresa Rogers: Kari-Lynn Winters, Mia Perry, and Anne-Marie LaMonde were doctoral students at the time we began the project and are now deeply involved in work in schools, universities, and communities. The project would not have been possible without their amazing skills and talents in working and researching with young people.

Thank you to my sons, Shaun and Christopher, who helped us with this project at various points. Shaun helped with the video production at LOVE and both have helped with technical aspects of data organization. They also served more or less willingly at various points as youth informants. My husband Rob's support is too extensive to delineate. He has listened and provided comments and insights all these years and will likely be happy this book is now done.

I also want to acknowledge funding from the Social Sciences and Humanities Council of the Government of Canada, as well as additional funding from the John and Doris Andrews Research and Development Award from the University of British Columbia Faculty of Education.

Kari-Lynn Winters: I would like to thank the following people: Eli, Renata, and Colin, staff and facilitators at the center for street youth during the project; Jonah Winters, for his editorial help; the Gathering Place and Family Services of Greater

Vancouver; Gumboot books (for their support in creating the design of the poetry chapbook), and the youth themselves.

Mia Perry: Thank you, Terry, for the opportunity to be involved with this rich project from its inception. Thank you also to the fifteen students at Lismore Secondary who welcomed me so readily into their classroom week after week. They stepped far outside their comfort zones, and bravely altered their expectations and assumptions of theatre.

Anne-Marie LaMonde: Working with Terry, my doctoral peers, and the youth was a fantastic experience. I enjoyed every discursive moment, especially within our small group of investigators as we tried to find intersections between the projects. The youth with whom I journeyed for a time at LOVE were, of course, truly inspiring. Their stories, wildness, spirit, talents, joys, and sorrows plunged me into uncommon reflection. I will be forever grateful to have had the extraordinary opportunity of being part of a memorable project with such exuberant and committed participants.

Chapter 4 is a revised and expanded version of M. Perry and T. Rogers, (2011), Meddling with "drama class," muddling "urban": Imagining aspects of the urban feminine self through an experimental theatre process with youth, in *Research in Drama Education: The Journal of Applied Theatre*, special issue: Drama and Theatre in Urban Contexts, *16*(2) 197–213.

1

YOUTH LITERACIES

Arts, Media, and Critical Literacy Practices as Civic Engagement

We know what's going on and we're trying to change it.

This quote is from a seventeen-year-old girl in the YouthCLAIM project—the focus of this book. The project explored the ways adolescents and young adults from diverse urban settings in Vancouver, Canada, use writing, visual arts, film, and theatre to make critical claims about their everyday lived experiences. Some of the youth faced the challenges of living on and off the streets, some were speaking back to the violence in their lives and our society, and others were exploring the intersection of their lived adolescent experiences and imagined futures. We describe and analyze their resulting cultural productions by looking closely at what events, practices, ideas, and ideologies the youth creatively explored and incisively critiqued within their communities as well as their contribution to the larger ongoing projects of collective democratic life and social justice. We used the title Youth-CLAIM in our project to suggest an alternative set of truth claims offered by the youth—claims that interrupt larger cultural discourses about youth, particularly about diverse or variously marginalized youth in our society.

This book builds upon and extends recent work on the communicative possibilities of "new literacies" (Lankshear and Knobel, 2003; Coiro et al., 2008), and contemporary perspectives of critical youth studies (e.g., Talburt and Lesko, 2012; Fine, Tuck, and Yang, 2014; Ibrahim and Steinberg, 2014). By describing the new and critical literacies of these youth through "the epistemology of the particular" (Stake, 2005), we illustrate how they exploit these resources at the intersection of local and global discourses, and how their practices, as form of civic engagement or public pedagogy, include cultural critique and speak to contemporary societal transformations related to youth, media, and society (cf. Luke, 1995, 2003; Giroux,

2000). We argue that the youth described in these pages, through their arts, media, and literacy practices, are participating in a larger project of citizenship in uncertain times.

We understand citizenship as including what Berlant (2007) defines as a relationship between a nation's legal control and the presumption that citizens should have some limited autonomy in the form of control over their lives and bodies, which the nation protects. However, these promises have been delivered unevenly and often in service of the more powerful segments of society. We are therefore exploring the claims of the youth in these pages as expressions of resistance to the inheritance of the broken promises of democratic citizenship and their ability to imagine new possibilities for public engagement.

The YouthCLAIM Project

We began our YouthCLAIM (Youth Critical Literacies and Arts-Integrated Media) project wondering what it might look like to work with youth in diverse settings in Vancouver, Canada, as they took up the multiple and creative resources of arts, media, and literacy to make claims about their lives. As in previous research, this project began in response to requests to collaborate from teachers and community educators working with youth, arts, and media (Rogers, 2009; Rogers and Schofield, 2005; Rogers, Winters, LaMonde, and Perry, 2010; Schofield and Rogers, 2004). We were contacted by three very different groups with ideas for collaborating on a project: an administrator in a center that provided resources for street-entrenched youth was looking for literacy and technology resources; a program coordinator for a community youth anti-violence program was interested in extending a photo journalism course with video production; and a school drama teacher wanted to experiment with new and multimodal forms of theatre. The youth we worked with ranged in age from fourteen up to twenty-six and represented a variety of ethnic and cultural identities; they faced economic realities that included being homeless and out of school to living in working- or middle-class homes and attending school full time.

Vancouver, Canada, and its surrounding areas ("metro Vancouver") has a population of approximately 2.4 million people. It is still largely comprised of people from European backgrounds, predominantly from Britain, Ireland, and Germany, while Chinese are the largest visible minority group. Vancouver has experienced a 50 percent growth rate increase from 2006 to 2011. It is the third largest city in Canada, with a 40 percent immigrant population; over half of recent immigrants emigrated from India, China, and the Philippines (Metro Vancouver, 2014). First Nations people make up approximately 2 percent of the population.

Like many contemporary cities there is and has been a large and growing disparity between rich and poor with a relatively stable middle class. Since the mid-1990s there has been a surge in development along with gentrification and dislocation as forces of immigration, geography, and capitalism have resulted in a severe shortage of affordable housing. Vancouver is also well-known for its visible homeless population of nearly 2,800 people in the metro Vancouver region, including over four hundred youth and a disproportionately high number of First Nations people, who make up nearly a third of the homeless people (Jackson, 2014; Sinoski, 2014).

As a city, Vancouver shares many of the characteristics of the modern global or world city (Crossette, 2001; Massey, 2007) in neoliberal times and is marked by increasing privatization of public goods; cutbacks in social services; sectorization by differences in race, class, ethnicity, and culture; hyper-gentrification of the housing market; and attendant rise in poverty. Within Vancouver is the Downtown Eastside (DTES)—a catchment area for the city, province, and nation for homeless people dealing with addiction, engaging as sex trade workers, and so on (see Figures 1.1 and 1.2).

FIGURE 1.1 Images of Vancouver, photos taken by Tweek, a street youth

FIGURE 1.2 Images of Vancouver, photos taken by Tweek, a street youth

FIGURE 1.3 Image of Olympic cauldron in Vancouver, photo taken by Max Paq

Credit: Maxime Paquin

In fact, the DTES has been referred to as "Canada's poorest postal code" (City of Vancouver, 2005–2006). The DTES has been discursively produced and repro-duced as a kind of "cautionary tale" in the popular imagination, both locally and globally, and forms a persistent backdrop to the everyday lives of the youth in the project. This was particularly the case at the time of this project as the world gaze was turning toward Vancouver as the site of the 2010 Olympics (see Figure 1.3).

As with most projects that include educational researchers who enter communities and schools, there were some initial differences in purpose and goals as well as rich exchanges. As much as possible we listened to the youth and mentors in their sites to discover what they wanted to learn and accomplish and how we might support them. The university research team included the co-authors of this volume, each of whom contributed her own unique talents to the development of the arts-integrated media projects at one site.

Because each of the yearlong projects was negotiated on site, they were also distinct. Kari-Lynn Winters and I worked with a zine program with homeless or street-involved youth, which integrated creative writing and visual arts; Anne-Marie LaMonde and I worked on a video production project with youth who were advocating against violence; and Mia Perry and I worked with a teacher on an original devised theatre performance with secondary school drama students. As a team, we met to share approaches, read theoretical works, and discussed ways to analyze our ongoing work. A brief description of our work at each site follows.

The Centre for Homeless Youth

The zine (small-circulation magazine) project extended an already existing workshop that took place for two hours on one evening every week at a youth services center (see also Rogers and Winters, 2010). The center, located in the city core, strives to provide homeless or street-involved youth an entry point for accessing the support they need to make healthy and positive changes in their lives, and to change the larger community's perception of them. The center is open all the time (24/7) and provides food, a place to rest (but not sleep), counseling and peer support services, health services, employment and training, and a range of arts programs (music, arts, writing, dance, film). Most services are available to youth eighteen years and younger; however, workshops for *Another Slice* (the name of the zine) were open to youth up to twenty-four years of age. Many of those youth between the ages of eighteen and twenty-four attended the zine workshops initially to get snacks and an evening meal, which they were allowed to do if they participated.

We supported the youth as they created and produced their monthly zine, occasionally providing writing workshops, and supplying cameras, film developing, computers, printed copies of the zine, and other resources as needed. The zines were sold or given away on the streets and showcased at open houses. We eventually also helped them produce a poetry chapbook, *Voices from the Street* (Mills and Rogers, 2009) which included poems from the zine and additional submissions. Later we coproduced a set of films that speak to an academic and public audience about homelessness. The history of the zine in this site and our work with the youth each week over the course of a year is described in Chapter 2.

The Leave Out Violence (LOVE) Project

Within a Vancouver community center located on the east side of the city, this after-school anti-violence community program serves youth who are attending secondary school. This site is one of several in North America, with project locations in Montreal, Halifax, Toronto, and New York City. The purpose of LOVE is to help youth end violence in their lives and become community leaders of violence prevention. The program employs a range of media, including photography, video, broadcasting, and journalism to analyze and document the causes and effects of violence, and to propose solutions. They state: "LOVE youth use the media tools they create and the life skills they learn to promote non-violence youth-to-youth across cultural, political, racial, religious, socio-economic and geographical boundaries" (LOVE, 2013).

Our video project at the community anti-violence program extended an existing photojournalism project and provided the youth with new tools for expressing and sharing their experiences with violence. The youth met with us for two hours in the evening, once a week across a year, to learn filmmaking skills and develop individual and group video projects that were eventually shared at a public fundraising event. We describe our yearlong project at this site in Chapter 3.

The Secondary School Drama Program

The secondary school drama project took shape in a fairly large public secondary school in North Vancouver (Lismore Secondary School, a pseudonym). The school community consists of largely lower- and middle-income families and is located about five miles north of downtown Vancouver. We worked with a drama teacher and one of her ninth-grade classes using devised theatre approaches to creating theatrical scenes and performances. The teacher was interested in exploring this more contemporary approach to drama/theatre that combined creation and spectatorship. The material, or texts, for the ongoing work and performances were drawn from the real and imagined lives of the students (Perry and Rogers, 2011). The work opened up a space for contemporary adolescents situated on the boundaries of a city with complex cultural and social issues, to critique their coming-of-age experiences in a particular geographic location.

As a project that was distinct from the typical school drama curriculum, we explored how the youth used the multimodal and performative tools of theatre to explore a mix of interests, experiences (real and vicarious), themes related to representing adolescence that emerged through their play (with improvisations, characters, and scenes), spectatorship, and performances. As described in Chapter 4, we worked with the students and teacher two to three times a week across the academic year and the project culminated in a public performance at the school.

Theoretical Frameworks of Youth Literacies and Civic Engagement

Three key theoretical constructs guide our analyses and descriptions of cases within the project. These constructs, emanating from the intersection of theoretical frameworks described below, are multimodal intertextuality, cultural critique, and the range of public or civic engagements of the youth. That is, we are particularly interested in sharing the ways these contemporary youth skillfully used the tools and resources of literacy, arts, and media to create sophisticated multimodal texts that include incisive cultural critique to make public claims about their lives and society.

Multimodal Intertextuality

Much of the early work in multiple and critical adolescent literacies contested the privileging of print literacies and supported hybrid and unsanctioned literacy practices in and out of classrooms (e.g., Moje, 2000; O'Brien, 2005). Researchers have more recently provided many examples of youth as producers of new forms of arts, literacy, and media as they comment on and critique their social worlds (e.g., Burn and Parker, 2003; Hill and Vasudevan, 2008; Hull and Nelson, 2005; Jocson, 2013; Morell, 2008; Rogers and Winters, 2010; Rogers, Winters, LaMonde, and Perry, 2010; Sanford, Rogers, and Kendrick, 2014; Sefton-Green, 2006; Soep, 2006; Vasudevan and DeJaynes, 2013).

As these many examples illustrate, new media resources bring with them new models of authorship, collaboration, intertextuality and remixing, and reveal youth to be flexible, playful, creative and critical users of genres and modalities, often appropriating, hybridizing, and transforming a range of cultural forms and resources (Bakhtin, 1986; Buckingham and Sefton-Green, 1994; Dyson, 2003; Lemke, 1995; Kearney, 2006; Kress, 2003; Manovich, 2001; Rogers and Tierney, 2002; Street, 1995). We argue that these new multimodal spaces of arts, literacy, and media provide a plasticity of form (Bakhtin, 1986, p. 3), which allow room for adaptation and experimentation required to express ideas in constantly changing societal contexts. Some scholars have argued that multimodality also allows for a fuller expression of emotion and human experience (Stein, 2004).

These processes are often referred to as remixing—in essence, taking cultural artifacts and combining and manipulating them into new kinds of texts. In this sense, remix is as old as human cultures and art itself, allowing for the repopulating of other texts with our own semantic and expressive intentions. However, with the advent of new digital tools, youth are engaging more and more in DIY production and remixing practices resulting in "endless hybridizations" (Knobel and Lankshear, 2011) of genre, form, content, and technique. Products of these new media and technologies illustrate the ways youth are engaging in recontextualization (Dyson, 2003) and a "robust dialogue" (Giroux, 2005, p. 25) with contemporary forms of meaning-making. In our work, we are particularly interested in the ways contemporary youth use these arts, media, literacy, and digital resources, playfully exploiting them as tools of sustained, creative, incisive, and public cultural critique in relation to critical social issues. As Hull (2103) points out, we are currently witnessing a new call for an aesthetic turn in education as a process of world-making and transforming social worlds.

To analyze multimodal intertextuality in the project we draw on theories of genre, form, and multimodal literacy practices to provide a focused lens for examining the ways youth engage in a rich use of modalities (print, drama, art, film, and so forth), and the ways they layer forms and genres as identity work in their quest to create meaning (Hull and Nelson, 2005; Kress and Van Leeuwen, 2001). We view genres as flexible cultural forms that exist in networks of relations of power and status, purposes of communication, and dialogue (e.g., Bakhtin, 1986; Lemke, 1995; Manovich, 2001; Street, 1995). Genres can also be seen as cultural practices that draw on intertextual strategies (Kristeva, 1980) to bridge or minimize gaps between discourses, allowing for "dialogical contact" (Bakhtin, 1986, p. 45 fn) and the production of new social power of expression (Biggs and Bauman, 1992).

Specifically, we were interested in the ways the youth in these sites exploited genres, modes, and practices in their work—juxtaposing and hybridizing and remixing these cultural forms, from reversing messages in corporate ads and playfully using public service announcement genres to performing revised fairy tales. In short, we set out to capture the kind of multimodal intertextual work the youth engaged in during the processes of writing, drawing, filming, and performing as well as how this work constitutes critical arts, media, and literacy practices and production.

Counter Narratives and Cultural Critique

We situate our work, in part, in the longstanding tradition of critical literacy and pedagogy of Paulo Freire, Henry Giroux, Allan Luke, Barbara Comber, Hillary Janks, and others, as well as contemporary critical media scholars (e.g., Douglas Kellner, Carmen Luke, Megan Boler, and others). Freire delineated a key distinction between systematic education, which can only be changed by those in power, and educational projects in which oppression can be transformed through "praxis" involving both a change in the way oppression is perceived and the "expulsion of myths" of the oppressor (Freire, 1970, pp. 54–55).

In many ways the work of the youth in this project represents a post-Freireian educational project in which they engage in a dialogue that names the everyday world around them, creating counter discourses or counter narratives (Giroux, Lankshear, McLaren, and Peters, 1996). As Foucault argued, when those usually spoken for or about by others begin to speak for themselves, they produce a "counter-discourse" (Foucault, 1977; cited in Moussa and Scapp, 1996, p. 89). These counter-narrative discourses resist and challenge the legitimacy of the original discourses, and "presuppose a horizon of competing, contrary utterances against which it asserts its own energies" (Terdiman, 1985, p. 36), thus forming a strong cultural critique.

The advent of new tools of literacy, arts, and media provides these youth with even more multimodal and discursive resources to participate in democratic society (Kellner and Share, 2007). Rather than focusing solely on media critique, this work engages youth in literacy, arts, and media production as creators of their own meanings: "they become subjects in the process of deconstructing injustices, expressing their own voices, and struggling to create a better society" (Kellner and Share, 2007, p. 20).

Contemporary poststructuralist, feminist, and spatial perspectives also inform our understanding of subjectivity and critical pedagogy in this project. Ellsworth (2005), for instance, theorizes places of learning as whole bodies/minds/selves in motion, and pedagogy as places of shared emergence and learning as knowledge and discourses are created and/or reconfigured. Within these pedagogical spaces, adolescent bodies contribute to the creation and representations of lived realities (Grosz, 1994; Merleau-Ponty, 1962); that is, the body is continually inscribed with, and generating information about, youth subjectivity and positioning (Ellsworth, 2005; Grosz and Eisenman, 2001).

In these rich pedagogical spaces youth in the three project sites poached texts and media and deployed parody, irony, and satire as critical and oppositional tactics across their productions. We define satire by drawing again on the work of Bakhtin. As he argued, meaning in literature is a function of the interaction among the author, the speaker in the text, and the reader/listener, "a dialogue among points of view" (Bakhtin, 1981). When these positions contrast, through the use of parody, for instance, it can result in satire that depicts conflicting social judgments (Stewart, 1983). Parody is created when an author is oriented not just to his or her subject or topic, but also to how that subject or topic is addressed by others through language or image—that is, a text about text. Youth often draw on popular culture and new media tools to engage in parody and other forms of satire in school contexts (Buckingham and Sefton-Green, 1994; Rogers, Winters, LaMonde, and Perry, 2010); in this project we were particularly impressed by the sophisticated uses of parody as public social critique.

Tactical uses of media, in particular, are often localized inventions of practices that contest dominant values and discourses, as opposed to "strategic" uses of media that uphold or perpetuate them. As researchers in the areas of literacy and media have observed, citizens on the margins of society often engage in similar tactical (DeCerteau, 1984) uses of public spaces—creatively borrowing or poaching popular culture texts and recombining rules and products for their own ends (Boler, 2008; Knobel and Lankshear, 2002). The use of irony, parody, and satire among youth in this project reflects these tactics and gives voice to their claims about homelessness, violence, and contemporary adolescent bodies and lives—lively counter narratives to dominant cultural discourses.

Public Pedagogy and Civic Engagement

We ultimately characterize these youth productions as a form of public pedagogy (Giroux, 2000; Sandlin, Schultz, and Burdick, 2010) and civic engagement. Thinking about this work as a public pedagogy helps us, as educators, to understand the connections among a range of formal and informal sites of learning and public life, and the role of "new literacies" in contemporary participatory culture (Jenkins et al., 2009). In all three of these projects, whether in a community or school setting, the youth produced work that made claims about control of their bodies and lives that were eventually taken into the public realm in the form of civic engagement, producing relationships with the public sphere. This occurred in both embodied places, including public viewings and performances, and digital spaces through publishing paper and online versions of a zine, a poetry anthology, and films about youth homelessness, creating and sharing videos about youth and anti-violence in a public forum, and creating an original theatre performance for a local school community.

In thinking about these productions, we note the intersections of the local and the global in such contemporary forms of cultural participation by drawing on contemporary discussions of media literacy, post-structural feminist theories, critical perspectives, and the work of cultural geographers. Youth participatory culture, according to Jenkins et al. (2009), includes producing and circulating content and creating a kind of "convergence culture" that can work to "repair the damage caused by an increasing privatized culture" (Jenkins et al., 2009, p. 256) or, we might add, offer alternatives to a more globalized and corporatized form of popular culture. In fact, the very notion of participatory culture is that new media provide new avenues and new spaces for youth to actively produce culture and participate in civic engagement both in and out of schools. Learning takes place in a variety of public spheres that allow us to connect the larger culture, the productions of youth, and the challenges of radical democracy in what Giroux (2005) calls "a newly constituted global public" (p. 9).

The concept of public pedagogy seeks to position "rigorous theoretical work and public bodies against corporate power, connect classrooms to the challenges faced by social movements in the streets, and provide spaces within classrooms for personal injury and private terrors to be translated into public considerations and struggles" (Giroux, 2001, p. xxx). Extending this concept, Sandlin et al. (2010) argue that public pedagogy requires a contextualized sensibility towards research and theorizing, drawing on a range of cultural discourses, while seeking "to inhabit complex and ambiguous spaces of pedagogical address" (p. 3). Our work with the youth in this project directly addresses such complex, impermanent, and ambiguous spaces of learning and takes us from the street to the community center to the classroom in seeking to support and engage with youth who are, through literacy, arts, and media, creatively and critically constructing counter narratives to normative cultural discourses and making public and critical claims about their bodies, their material lives, and society.

In looking closely at what youth say and do in one location, in relation to smaller and larger audiences, we begin to understand the circulation of ideas or cultural motion at the intersection of local and global discourses (Appadurai, 1996). In this way, our view of the local is very much connected to the global. As Bhabha (1996) would argue, and as we witnessed in our work with the youth, the local is continually "contaminated" by the global (p. 54), and the global cannot be conceived without attention to how it is produced/reproduced in the local in what Doreen Massey refers to as "constellations of temporary coherence" (1998, p. 125)—issues we illustrate throughout the descriptions of our work with the youth in the project and then take up in more depth in our conclusion.

Locating the "Youth" in Critical Youth Studies

We draw on contemporary assumptions about youth culture that resist notions of "the adolescent" as biological or a solely cognitive "stage" characterized as "unfinished" that diminish and limit adolescent bodies and subjectivities (e.g., Walkerdine, 1990; Vadenboncoeur, 2005; Lesko, 1996, 2012). We view youth culture as a rich, complex site with multiple possible affiliations within which particular youth, in what some describe as the "millennial generation," express intersecting subjectivities in a variety of critical expressions inscribed in their work and/or on their bodies. At each site, we indeed found complex and intersecting affiliations within the groups we worked with; for instance, the zine group included a range of identity positions within the larger categories of "street," "street-entrenched" or "homeless" youth (all variously used and rejected by the youth) such as self-identified "couch-surfers" (temporarily housed youth), "trainhoppers," "twinkies" (new to the street), and "tweekers" (drug users). Many of the youth also identified as poets, artists, or musicians, and performed various other intersecting subjectivities related to gender, ethnicity, sexuality, etc.

We also note, along with critical youth studies researchers (e.g., Cammarota and Fine, 2008), that youth are continuously engaged in analyzing their social and cultural contexts and both recognize and resist power in various ways. As part of this process, we found that youth may form momentary or more sustained coalitions across subject positions as they come together to produce zines, films, and performances and to engage in cultural critique. This work often draws on resistance to various cultural norms and practices, and at times works toward social change in ways that are fluid and unfixed, yet also have the potential to open up new possibilities.

Some of these productions resulted in contributing to "networked publics" (e.g., Ito, 2008)—online sites and networks as active participation in the public sphere, and others resulted in creating counterpublics (Fraser, 1990; Warner, 2002) or "little publics" (Hickey-Moody, 2013, p. 19)—live audiences that came together to hear and view the work of the youth, contributing to the possibilities for civic engagement, and even providing frameworks for policy. In this digital era, we concur with Hickey-Moody (2013) that it is essential to recognize the continuing importance of these little publics as modes of community attachment, forming a kind of aesthetic citizenship and potentially contributing to debates about the public good. We argue that, collectively, the youth we worked with are saying important things about the gentrification and growing material inequities of the contemporary global city, diminishing and inadequate institutional support systems, loss of recognizability and legitimacy, and new forms of youth identifications (Butler, 2009; Dillabough and Kennelly, 2010; Talburt and Lesko, 2012).

A Note on Research Methods

We conducted our project as a qualitative multi-site case study (Stake, 2005). As stated above, we were interested in the particular—how youth in specific sites took on the tools of literacy, arts, and media to make claims about homelessness, violence, and contemporary adolescence within one geographical area.

At each case study site we acted as participant-observers (Glesne and Peshkin, 1992), both supporting the youth work through various kinds of artistic support and instruction and provision of materials and observing their work. While with the youth, we often took "jottings" (Emerson, Fretz, and Shaw, 1995) rather than extended field notes depending on the site. We then expanded our jottings and field notes into more formal field notes after each session with a group. We occasionally audio- or videotaped meetings or classes at the LOVE and Lismore sites. Our formal field notes consisted of documenting the events that took place including remembered or jotted dialogue and then creating research memos around three key questions: What is of particular interest regarding the subjectivities/interests/cultures of the youth? How are the modes, forms, and genres of literacy, arts, and media used as resources? What critical and public work is being done?

Our participation at each site was specific to and negotiated with the youth and the program mentors. Engaging in projects such as this always raises interesting issues and dilemmas in relation to institutional ethics and site relationships. At the street youth site we began in the spring and we had to renegotiate our entry when a new youth worker took over in the autumn. Also at the street youth site, the administrator who originally invited us noted that our standard university consent forms were ill-suited to the context. She wrote to us: "I am worried about your consent form. You are using a parent/guardian model, which is not possible with our youth. Social workers won't sign these things. We will not sign them either. Researchers working with this population tend to get permission from the ethics board for youth to sign for themselves" (email from youth worker). We were eventually granted permission to have youth who were sixteen and over sign on their own behalf.

At the street youth site and the Leave Out Violence site there was also quite a bit of transience so we had to be flexible with any ongoing project plans depending on who showed up that evening. At the secondary school site there was much more regular attendance but our relationship with the teacher and our role in the creation and production of a devised theatre performance, which was a fairly radical experiment for a school curriculum, was extremely labor intensive, required constant renegotiation as the academic year progressed.

At the zine site with homeless youth, we listened in as they ran the meeting and visitors conducted workshops, provided our own support for creative writing and visual art, provided cameras, and assisted with publishing and other public outreach activities. We paid for food at the meetings and offered twenty dollars to youth who were willing to be interviewed about their zine work. At the anti-violence site we ran initial workshops on filming, led discussions of film critique, provided suggestions for film topics, approaches, and genres, provided technical support and equipment for film production, and supported the development of a final film montage for a public fundraising event. At the school theatre site, we taught contemporary performance creation skills, provided the students with an opportunity to view live professional contemporary theatre performances and discuss them, and worked with them to develop scenes and a final original theatre performance. A description of our approach to arts pedagogy (multimodal writing, film, and performance) and how we worked at each site is provided in the Appendix.

At each project site, we collected artifacts that the youth produced, including writing, artwork, films, scripts, photographs, and films—samples of which are evident throughout the book or available for viewing at the accompanying website: http://blogs.ubc.ca/theresarogersresearch/. We also interviewed between six and eight focal youth at each site, and many of their comments are also included throughout this volume. In these interviews, we asked them about their own preferences related to literacy, arts, and media; their responses to the activities/projects at each site; their respective roles in the work; and their reflections on specific pieces (writing, art, film, performance).

Our approach shares many of the commitments of youth participatory action research (Cammarota and Fine, 2008). These commitments include contesting popular assumptions about youth as delinquent, at-risk, undeveloped adults, etc. and the way societal structures create inequalities for young people. It includes a cycle of critical inquiry, and includes participation, inviting varied audiences, and a commitment to democratic practices. In all three sites, while our roles and level of participation varied, we remained in the first place committed to the completion of the project as initially conceived with the youth and the mentors at the site, particularly helping with the support of the work as it was shared with various audiences.

The major theoretical frames of this book were developed over time through a dialectic (Stake, 2005) between the findings at each case/project site and the overarching questions and ideas that kept arising as answers to our more theoretical memos in relation to the subjectivities, creative multimodal productions, and critical and public work of the youth.

Analytical Approach of the Book

Drawing on our previous work with youth and media production (Rogers, Winters, LaMonde, and Perry, 2010), we developed an analytic approach toward the process that focused on three sites of meaning-making. Adapted from the work of cultural geographer Gillian Rose (2001, 2007), we define these meaning-making sites as the intersecting sites of production, of the produced image (or text), and of audience.

Our corresponding pedagogical approach was to support the youth at the site of production by focusing on preparing through generating material and ideas; supporting a process of inquiry as they gathered and combined resources to move toward the site of the production itself; helping them to reflect by unpacking the material in ways that were suited to the arts or media context and product; and supporting them at the site of audience by helping them to further develop or reframe their work for intended readers and viewers (see Appendix). Our pedagogy with the street youth was the least structured, and the work with the drama students the most structured, consistent with the level of formality of the respective programs. We note that we provided this support as needed or requested; at times the youth independently produced writings, art, media, and performances.

Structure of the Book

We begin Chapters 2, 3, and 4 with extended vignettes to illustrate the particular ways we worked with or supported the youth in each site and to capture some of their textual, critical, and public claims in relation to the larger theme of the chapter. These vignettes, which show how youth appropriate the discursive resources of arts, media, and literacy to make claims about their bodies and lives, are descriptive and necessarily highly constructed stories based on our observations and field notes, and on our collection of documents and interviews. As university researchers, we recognize the power differential that is particularly pronounced when privileged academics enter the world of youth, and we acknowledge the ways in which this is our interpretation, containing some combination of our voices and those of the youth, in unequal measure. However, we provide these constructed vignettes as one window into the research sites so that our analysis of the work can be interpreted and evaluated by readers with some sense of what we saw, heard, and did in service of supporting the youth and their arts, media, and literacy productions, without attempt to erase power differentials. While we present the vignettes in a fairly linear fashion, the process was often more recursive and often partial or unfinished, depending on the interests, presence, and inclinations of the youth at each site.

Descriptions of the program at each site follow the introductory vignettes. We then explore a range of youth productions as examples of multimodal intertextuality, as cultural critique, and as public pedagogy. We theorize the youth work through the underlying lens of the sites of production, image, and audience, looking closely at their situated work together with our observations and conversations with them. While we emphasize the discursive and community engagements of these youth, we recognize and temper our analyses with an awareness of their respective levels of precarity and marginalization, from the edge of the urban core (Dillabough and Kennelly, 2010) to their role in the institution of schooling. Across the middle chapters of the book we move from the most precariously positioned youth, the street youth, to the school site, in effect moving from the urban core to the more peripheral or proximal neighborhood, though we argue that the urban imaginary of Vancouver is present across these sites.

Final Word

We began this project as young (and older) people were gathering in cities around the world to protest against social injustice related to years of economic inequality and the tensions between the promise of democracy and the perversions of unregulated capitalism (e.g., Occupy Wall Street). These moments of resistance are important and happen in small and large ways, they wax and wane, and continue in various interconnecting trajectories. As the world continues to grapple with social and economic inequalities and injustices, we believe we should train our eyes on the ways in which youth, as civic actors, become increasingly involved in these various forms of political and cultural engagement and critique and to find ways to support those efforts. In particular, our hope is that this book will contribute to and extend current conversations about the lively intersections among youth arts, literacy, and media production, pedagogy, and social justice.

References

Appadurai, A. (1996). *Modernity at large: Cultural dimensions of globalization.* Minneapolis: University of Minneapolis Press.

Bakhtin, M. M. (1981). *The dialogic imagination: Four essays by M. M. Bakhtin.* (Trans. C. Emerson & M. Holquist). Austin: University of Texas Press.

Bakhtin, M. M. (1986). *Speech genres and other late essays.* Austin: University of Texas Press.

Berlant, L. (2007). Citizenship. In B. Burgett & G. Hendler (Eds.), *Keywords for American cultural studies* (pp. 37–42). New York: NYU Press.

Bhabha, H. (1996). Culture's in-between. In S. Hall & P. du Gay (Eds.), *Questions of cultural identity* (pp. 53–60). Thousand Oaks, CA: Sage.

Biggs, C., & Bauman, R. (1992). Genre, intertextuality and social power. *Journal of Linguistic Anthropology, 2*(2), 131–172.

Boler, M. (2008). *Digital media and democracy.* Toronto: University of Toronto Press.

Buckingham, D., & Sefton-Green, J. (1994). *Cultural studies goes to school.* Bristol: Taylor & Francis.

Burn, A., & Parker, D. (2003). *Analysing media texts.* London: Continuum.

Butler, J. (2009). Performativity, precarity and sexual politics. *Revista de Antropología Iberoamericana, 4*(3), i–xiii.

Cammarota, J., & Fine, M. (2008). Youth participatory action research: A pedagogy for transformational resistance. In J. Cammarota & M. Fine (Eds.), *Revolutionizing education: Youth participatory action research in motion* (pp. 1–12). New York: Routledge.

City of Vancouver. (2005–2006). *Downtown Eastside community monitoring report. Downtown Eastside revitalization* (10th ed.). Retrieved from http://vancouver.ca/commsvcs/planning/dtes/2014/03/18

Coiro, J., Knobel, M., Lankshear, C., & Leu, D. (2008). Central issues in new literacies and new literacies research. In J. Coiro, M. Knobel, C. Lankshear, & D. Leu (Eds.), *Handbook of research on new literacies* (pp. 1–22). New York: Lawrence Erlbaum Associates.

Crossette, B. (2001, November 26). Canada's global city (not Toronto). *The New York Times*. Retrieved from http://www.nytimes.com/2001/11/26/world/canada-s-global-city-not-toronto.html

DeCerteau, M. (1984). *The practice of everyday life*. Berkeley: University of California Press.

Dillabough, J., & Kennelly, J. (2010). *Lost youth in the global city: Class, culture and the urban imaginary*. New York: Routledge.

Dyson, A. H. (2003). *The brothers and sisters learn to write: Popular literacies in childhood and school cultures*. New York: Teachers College Press.

Ellsworth, E. (2005). *Places of learning: Media architecture pedagogy*. New York: RoutledgeFalmer.

Emerson, R., Fretz, R., & Shaw, L. (1995). *Writing ethnographic fieldnotes*. Chicago, IL: University of Chicago Press.

Fine, M., Tuck, E., & Yang, K. W. (2014). An intimate memoir of resistance theory. In E. Tuck & K. W. Yang (Eds.), *Youth resistance research and theories of change* (pp. 46–58). New York: Routledge.

Foucault, M. (1977). Nietzsche, genealogy, history. In D. F. Bouchard (Ed.), *Language, counter-memory, and practice* (pp. 139–164). Ithaca: Cornell University Press.

Fraser, N. (1990). Rethinking the public sphere: A contribution to the critique of actually existing democracy. *Social Text, 25/26*, 56–80.

Freire, P. (1970). *Pedagogy of the oppressed*. New York: Continuum.

Giroux, H. (2000). Public pedagogy as cultural politics: Stuart Hall and the "crisis" of culture. *Cultural Studies, 14*(2), 341–360.

Giroux, H. (2001). Introduction: Educated hope, public pedagogy and the politics of resistance. In *Theory and Resistance in Education: Towards a Pedagogy for the Opposition*. Santa Barbara, CA: Praeger.

Giroux, H. (2005). Cultural studies in dark times: Public pedagogy and the challenge of neoliberalism. *Fast capitalism, 1*(2). Retrieved September 6, 2014, from http://fastcaptitalism.com

Giroux, H., Lankshear, C., McLaren, P., & Peters, M. (Eds.). (1996). *Counternarratives: Cultural studies and critical pedagogies in postmodern spaces*. New York: Routledge.

Glesne, C., & Peshkin, A. (1992). *Becoming qualitative researchers: An introduction*. New York: Longman.

Grosz, E. (1994). *Volatile bodies: Toward a corporeal feminism*. Bloomington: Indiana University Press.

Grosz, E., & Eisenman, P. (2001). *Architecture from the outside: Essays on virtual and real space*. Cambridge, MA: MIT Press.

Hickey-Moody, A. (2013). *Youth, arts and education: Reassembling subjectivity through affect*. New York: Routledge.

Hill, M. L., & Vasudevan, L. (2008). *Media, literacy and sites of possibility*. New York: Routledge.

Hull, G. (2013). Foreword: Visible youth. In L. Vasudevan & T. DeJaynes (Eds.), *Arts, media and social justice· Multimodal explorations with youth* (pp. ix–xii). New York: Peter Lang.

Hull, G., & Nelson, M. E. (2005). Locating the semiotic power of multimodality. *Written Communication, 22,* 224–261.

Ibrahim, A., & Steinberg, D. (2014). *Critical youth studies reader.* New York: Peter Lang.

Ito, M. (2008). Introduction. In K. Varnelis (Ed.), *Networked publics* (pp. 1–14). Cambridge, MA: MIT Press.

Jackson, E. (2014, April 23). Street homelessness doubles in Vancouver. *Vancouver Metro.* Retrieved from http://metronews.ca/news/vancouver/1011497/vancouver-homeless-population-nearly-doubles-in-2014/

Jenkins, H., Purushotma, R., Weigel, M., Clinton, K., & Robison, A. J. (2009). *Confronting the challenges of participatory culture: Media education for the 21st century.* Cambridge, MA: MIT Press.

Jocson, K. M. (2013). Remix revisited: Critical solidarity in youth media arts. *E–Learning and Digital Media, 10*(1), 68–82.

Kearney, M. (2006). *Girls make media.* New York: Routledge.

Kellner, D., & Share, J. (2007). Critical media literacy, democracy, and the reconstruction of education. In D. Macedo & S. R. Steinberg (Eds.), *Media literacy: A reader* (pp. 3–23). New York: Peter Lang.

Knobel, M., & Lankshear, C. (2002). Cut, paste, publish: The production and consumption of zines. In D. Alvermann (Ed.), *Adolescents and literacies in a digital world* (pp. 164–185). New York: Peter Lang.

Knobel, M., & Lankshear, C. (2011). Remix: The art and craft of endless hybridization. *Journal of Adolescent & Adult Literacy, 52*(1), 22–33.

Kress, G. (2003). *Literacy in the new media age.* London: Routledge.

Kress, G., & Van Leeuwen, T. (2001). *Multimodal discourse: The modes and media of contemporary communication.* New York: Oxford University Press.

Kristeva, J. (1980). *Desire in language: A semiotic approach to literature and art.* New York: Columbia University Press.

Lankshear, C., & Knobel, M. (2003). *New literacies: Changing knowledge and classroom learning.* Berkshire, UK: Open University Press.

Lemke, J. (1995). *Textual politics.* London: Taylor and Francis.

Lesko, N. (1996). Denaturalizing adolescence: The politics of contemporary representations. *Youth and Society, 28*(2), 139–161.

Lesko, N. (2012). *Act your age! A cultural construction of adolescence* (2nd ed.). New York: Routledge.

LOVE. (2013). About LOVE. Retrieved April 10, 2014, from http://leaveoutviolence.org/

Luke, C. (1995). Media literacy and cultural studies. In P. Freebody, S. Muspratt, & A. Luke (Eds.), *Constructing critical literacies* (pp. 19–50). Crosskill, NJ: Hampton Press.

Luke, C. (2003). Pedagogy, connectivity, multimodality, and interdisciplinarity. *Reading Research Quarterly, 38*(3), 397–403.

Manovich, L. (2001). *The language of new media.* Cambridge, MA: MIT Press.

Massey, D. (1998). The spatial construction of youth cultures. In T. Skelton & G. Valentine (Eds.), *Cool places: Geographies of youth cultures* (pp. 121–129). London: Routledge.

Massey, D. (2007). *World city.* London: Polity.

Merleau-Ponty, M. (1962). *Phenomenology of perception.* Evanston, IL: Northwestern University Press.

Metro Vancouver. (2014). Immigration and cultural diversity (MV 20011 National Household Survey Bulletin #6). Retrieved from http://www.metrovancouver.org/about/publications/Publications/2011CensusNo6-ImmigrationCulturaDiverstiyl.pdf

Mills, E., & Rogers, T. (Eds.). (2009). *Words from the street: Writings from* Another Slice. Vancouver: SPN Publishing.

Moje, E. (2000). "To be part of the story": The literacy practices of gangsta adolescents. *Teachers College Record, 102*(3), 651–690.

Morrell, E. (2008). *Critical literacy and urban youth: Pedagogies of access, dissent, and liberation.* New York: Routledge.

Moussa, M., & Scapp, R. (1996). The practical theorizing of Michel Foucault: Politics and counter-discourse. *Cultural Critique, 33*, 87–112.

O'Brien, D. (2005). "At-risk" adolescents: Redefining competence through the multiliteracies of intermediality, visual arts, and representation. *Reading Online, 4*(11). Retrieved from http://www.readingonline.org/newliteracies/obrien/

Perry, M., & Rogers, T. (2011). Meddling with "drama class," muddling "urban": Imagining aspects of the urban feminine self through an experimental theatre process with youth. *Research in Drama Education: The Journal of Applied Theatre*, special issue: Drama and Theatre in Urban Contexts, *16*(2), 197–213.

Rogers, T. (2009). Theorizing media productions as complex literacy performances among youth in and out of schools. In D. Pullen & D. Cole (Eds.), *Handbook of research on multiliteracies and technology enhanced education* (pp. 133–146). Hershey, PA: IGI.

Rogers, T., & Schofield, A. (2005). Things thicker than words: Portraits of youth multiple literacies in an alternative secondary program. In J. Anderson, M. Kendrick, T. Rogers, & S. Smythe (Eds.), *Portraits of literacy across families, communities and schools* (pp. 205–220). Mahwah, NJ: Lawrence Erlbaum Associates.

Rogers, T., & Tierney, R. (2002). Intertextuality. In B. Guzzetti (Ed.), *Literacy in America: An encyclopedia of history, theory, and practice* (p. 258). Santa Barbara, CA: ABC-CLIO.

Rogers, T., & Winters, K. (2010). Textual play, satire, and counter discourses of street youth 'zining practices. In D. Alvesmann (Ed.), *Adolescents' online literacies: Connecting classrooms, digital media, and popular culture* (pp. 91–108). New York: Peter Lang.

Rogers, T., Winters, K., LaMonde, A. M., & Perry, M. (2010). From image to ideology: Analysing shifting identity positions of marginalized youth across the cultural sites of video production. *Pedagogies: An International Journal, 5*(4), 298–312.

Rose, G. (2001). *Visual methodologies.* London: Sage.

Rose, G. (2007). *Visual methodologies* (2nd ed.). London: Sage.

Sandlin, J., Schultz, B. D., & Burdick, J. (Eds.). (2010). *Handbook of public pedagogy.* New York: Routledge.

Sanford, K., Rogers, T., & Kendrick, M. (Eds.). (2014). *Everyday youth literacies: Critical perspectives for new times.* New York: Springer Publications.

Schofield, A., & Rogers, T. (2004). At play in fields of ideas: Teaching, curriculum and the lives of youth. *Journal of Adolescent and Adult Literacies, 48*, 238–248.

Sefton-Green, J. (2006). Youth, technology and media cultures. In J. Green & A. Luke (Eds.), *Review of research in education* (pp. 279–306). Washington, DC: American Educational Research Association.

Sinoski, K. (2014, April 23). Number of people sleeping in Vancouver's streets or on couches more than tripled since 2011. *Vancouver Sun.* Retrieved from http://www.vancouversun.com/touch/news/metro/Majority+Metro+homeless+still+Vancouver+count+shows/9767325/story.html?rel=813152

Soep, E. (2006). Beyond literacy and voice in youth media production. *McGill Journal of Education, 41*(3), 197–214.

Stake, R. E. (2005). *Multiple case study analysis.* New York: Guilford Press.

Stein, P. (2004). Representation, rights, and resources: Multimodal pedagogies in the language and literacy classroom. In B. Norton & K. Toohey (Eds.), *Critical pedagogies and language learning* (pp. 95–115). Cambridge, UK: Cambridge University Press.

Stewart, S. (1983). Shouts on the street: Bakhtin's anti-linguistics. *Critical Inquiry, 10,* 265–281.

Street, B. (1995). *Social literacies: Critical approaches to literacy in development, ethnography and education.* New York: Longman.

Talburt, S., & Lesko, N. (2012). A history of the present of youth studies. In N. Lesko & S. Talburt (Eds.), *Keywords in youth studies: tracing affects, movements, knowledges.* New York: Routledge.

Terdiman, R. (1985). *Discourse/counter-discourse: Theory and practice of symbolic resistance in nineteenth century France.* Ithaca, NY: Cornell University Press.

Vadeboncoeur, J. A. (2005). Naturalized, restricted, packaged and sold: Reifying the fictions of "adolescent" and "adolescence." In J. Vadenboncoeur & L. Patel Stevens (Eds.), *Re/constructing "the adolescent": Sign, symbol and body* (pp. 1–24). New York: Peter Lang.

Vasudevan, L., & De Jaynes, T. (Eds.). (2013). *Arts, media and social justice: Multimodal explorations with youth.* New York: Peter Lang.

Walkerdine, V. (1990). *Schoolgirl fictions.* New York: Verso.

Warner, M. (2002). Publics and counterpublics. *Public Culture, 14*(1), 49–90.

2

SHOUTING FROM THE STREET

Youth, Homelessness, and Zining Practices

People on the streets do more than shoot up and fall down all day.
Jordan, a street youth in the zine program

We begin this and the next two chapters with vignettes to illustrate the kind of work we did with the youth at each site. At the center for street or homeless youth[1] anywhere between a handful and twenty or more youth, ages sixteen to twenty-six, showed up on Sunday evenings in the art room to contribute to the zine and eat pizza. On the particular evening described further on, Jordan, a twenty-six-year-old self-described "train hopper," was there, though he attended the zine meetings at the youth service center sporadically. The black toque, bearded face, and 16mm black earplug that Jordan wore were an integral part of his image and identity. On his hands, the letters STAND PROUD were tattooed, one letter per finger, above his knuckles.

Jordan wanted to participate in the zine program, to help him "get off the drink." He also wanted to create and submit a piece for the zine itself so that he could feel like a contributing member and tell others about his life and the subculture of train hoppers. He expressed interest in poetry because "so much can be said with so few words." He liked the "condensed-ness" that the poetic genre affords. Yet, he also indicated that he wasn't a strong writer and that he often felt "limited by his reading/writing abilities."[2]

Mike, a street youth attending the zine program, is talking loudly about how the city has differing agendas (in regard to a city-wide garbage strike that is happening at this time). Mike asks the group, "Whose agenda should count?" Then he mentions an idea that he has based on this issue—that Vancouver is getting a heroin shot because of the garbage strike (referring to the discarded needles).

FIGURE 2.1 SYJA cart

Jordan, watching him, seems interested in the idea. He makes a muffled comment that the city would be lost without the SYJA—Street Youth Job Action group—who clean up rigs (needles) around the downtown core (see Figure 2.1).

Kari-Lynn, who is sitting with Jordan, begins to work with him. She asks Jordan where these rigs might be found. He tells her, "Any lit area, including alleys, courtyards, dumpsters, playgrounds . . ." When he mentions playgrounds he appears agitated. He shakes his head and tells her about how he recently found rigs at the bottom of slides on school playgrounds. Then he states, "Rigs belong in boxes. Keep the rigs away from my schools." He is suggesting that users are either being careless by not putting their needles in the proper disposal boxes (see Figure 2.2) or they are purposely putting them there to prove to the city that the strike needs to end.

Kari-Lynn asks if this is a topic that he might like to write a poem about. He agrees, stating that people should know about this. Not knowing how much print-based literacy Jordan has or if he knows how to encode words—up until this point Jordan has only contributed photos—she asks him to suggest a list of places where he might find rigs. As he speaks, Kari-Lynn transcribes: "At the bottom of slides, waterfronts, fields, train yards, alleys, behind dumpsters, bushes, parking garages, playgrounds, or any lit area."

FIGURE 2.2 Needle disposal boxes

Kari-Lynn tells him that he has the beginning to his poem. He laughs and tells her that it's just a list, not a poem. She suggests that he draw a rig. He picks up the pen and begins drawing a thick, stout rig. He's not happy with the drawing and folds it up. He stashes it in his pocket. She tells him that they can draw another and that he can create what is called a concrete poem, using the words to frame the picture. Kari-Lynn shows an example, using a snake. He nods and then gathers his belongings (a well-worn backpack). As he leaves, he says "I could do this or I might just take pictures with the camera." Kari-Lynn nods.

Jordan returns to the program on October 21. He shows Kari-Lynn a paper and states, "I asked my friend to redraw a rig for me so that I can finish my poem for the zine." She suggests they get to work, asking who should print the words, you or me? He asks if Kari-Lynn will do it. At this point she is still unsure of his writing skills.[3] However, right after she finishes printing the prior list around the rig (see Figure 2.3), he takes the pen and writes, "Rigs go in a BOX: *NOT* in *my* parks and schools."

Then he underlines the words "NOT" and "my." Figure 2.3 includes this poem, which is eventually made into a zine page along with an irreverent photograph.

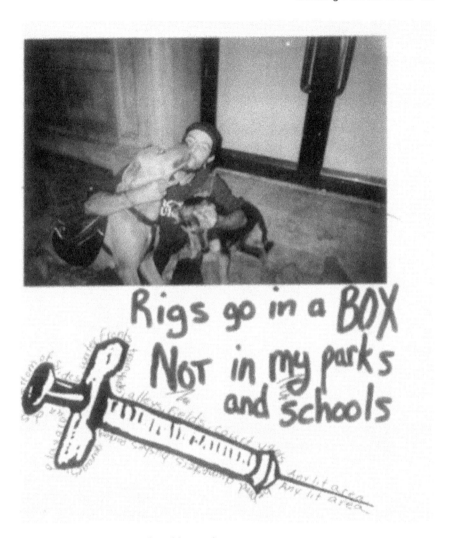

Rigs go in a BOX
Not in my parks
and schools

FIGURE 2.3 Zine page produced by Jordan

Others notice what Jordan is doing. A conversation emerges about how rigs are being found in the dumpsters and in the garbage cans. WB, another youth, mentions a mural that had been designed (see Figure 2.4) for the youth's smoking area.

In this mural, a rig can be seen in the garbage. This appears to infuriate Jordan. He talks about how the mural covered up his deceased friend's tags (graffiti writing). Others mention their annoyance as well. The talk around this mural and rigs in the garbage bins sets in motion a discussion that reflects the anxiety surrounding the issue of discarded rigs among the youth; some say that this mural is a trigger for further drug use.

FIGURE 2.4 Smoking room mural design

Credit: Kari-Lynn Winters

Before Jordan leaves, he takes out a small black photo book that he carries with him. He pulls out a picture of himself and his dogs, where he is giving the finger to the camera operator. He grabs a glue stick, slaps the glue on the back of the photo, sticks it to the page, and says: "Here's my submission [for the zine]."

We began this chapter with this vignette focusing on Jordan from the center for street youth zine workshop to illustrate how he took up the more familiar modalities of photography and drawing as well as declarative writing to create a new form of subjective critical expression and civic engagement. When we introduced him to a poetry form—concrete poetry—Jordan was able to combine these modalities to create a poster as a zine page effectively critiquing drug-related behaviors in his community.

Jordan drew on his own experiences and views about the behaviors of drug users in the city, along with the opinions of his peers, as a starting point for the production of his zine page. The zine format as a DIY communicative medium can be authored through multiple modes (linguistic, pictorial, photographic) and a variety of genres (e.g., poetry, visual art, announcements, interviews, essays). The flexibility provided Jordan with a set of discursive resources and tools to establish independence and to make his claims about something important to him. The page reflects a layering of these modes that result in a hybrid form that, like a contemporary poster, uses persuasive tactics along with an economy of language afforded by his concrete poem and slogan to address consumers of drugs in the

FIGURE 2.5 Sample cover from the original *Slice*

city. In the context of other related signs (such as the rig box in Figure 2.2) this poster participates in the urban "theatre of persuasion" (Sontag, 1999, pp. 196–197), providing a discursive bridge between Jordan's embodied experiences and his more publicly voiced opinions and concerns.

Within that message, he locates himself as a member of the community ("*my parks and schools*") he is addressing—a member who is concerned about the safety issues of children and others. The addition of the photograph adds another layer of identity positioning that may work with or against the poster genre below it, depending on how a viewer might "read" the assemblages of meaning, moving across the various modes (Winters, 2010). In addition, in the issue of this zine, Jordan's page sits between other pages of photographs taken by youth depicting scenes of their lives or from the city, poetic prose about addiction, and poems about homelessness, offering even more possible readings of Jordan's page.

Jordan's sense of his audience is evident in an interview in which he talked about his memories of the original version of the zine (then called *Slice*) that had run for several years during the late 1980s and the 1990s (see Figure 2.5).[4]

> Originally I had the idea to start the zine again last year. During the old *Slice* I was a young kid coming up on the street. Street kids didn't have much back then and this is something they can do. I'm a pretty outspoken person—[I'll talk about] anything I can argue a point for—like confrontation [or]

religion, for instance . . . I don't care about the reaction. If it's offered, that's cool. Street people are interested in writing, and art and shit like that. People on the streets do more than shoot up and fall down all day.

The zine afforded an opportunity for Jordan and others to express their ideas and create counter narratives to the discourses about street people. It provided safe spaces to voice opinions and "argue a point." Yet at the same time, Jordan expressed ambivalent interest in the nature of a public response—"I don't care about the reaction," he said, as he slammed down the photo at the end of a session (described above), yet he insisted his work be included in the zine.

Throughout the project we explored the role of the zine and other youth productions (e.g., a video series, a visual art gallery exhibit, a chapbook launch and reading) as sites of public engagement. The youth services coordinator who oversaw the zine program at the time, Eli, who was himself a former street youth, commented that he had read the old zines that Jordan referred to and were still around. Eli thought the zine was "amazing" and that it "gives voice to those who don't usually have a voice." He explained that the audience was initially seen to be other organizations, funders, and business improvement associations, but "now it's youth. *For youth, by youth*. They [the youth] give copies to each other here and in other safe houses. They have a local sense of audience and don't expect the establishment to read it . . . they use it for outreach. They don't want to have to sell them on the street but sometimes they do instead of panhandling."

In fact, many street youth talked about living their lives in the city within what one youth referred to as a "fourteen-block" radius—an area they knew well. They knew how to navigate within this area to stay safe; for instance, it included a flat space to leave their shopping carts and a bridge where they often slept, calling its underside their "sanctuary." Researchers have noted that spaces that are perceived to be safe (family homes) or that are created for homeless youth (such as shelters) are often viewed as less safe than public spaces where they have peer communities and networks (Rachlis, Wood, Zhang, Montaner, and Kerr, 2009; Wager, 2014).

Valuing the *localness* of their community was shared by most of the youth; the zine was primarily created and disseminated locally. However, later in the project when their sphere of communication broadened to a wider audience, there was a keen and continuing sense of creating first-hand "little publics" (Hickey-Moody, 2013, p. 19), especially for the distribution of their work to peers, social workers, politicians, academics, and policy-makers, or those local people that they felt contributed to the public good.

The extended vignette opening this chapter focused on one young man from the youth services center zine workshop. It illustrates, in a very particular way, how youth in this project appropriated the discursive resources of arts, media, and literacy to make larger public claims about their lived experiences and their worlds, critique their communities, and actively participate in civic engagement. By taking up the more familiar modalities of photography, drawing, and poetry, Jordan created a contemporary poster-like zine page to publicly admonish the careless drug-related behaviors of users in his community, a clear counter narrative to the larger, more stereotyped cultural discourses of street-entrenched youth. We now widen our focus back to zines themselves, to the program, and our yearlong project with Jordan and the other youth participants in the project.

Another Slice Zine Program

During the year (March through to the following February) we spent at this site, nine issues of the zine, *Another Slice,* were produced, including some with themes: Halloween, tattoos, and social workers. Each issue included a range of genres and modal forms—poetry, art, photography, announcements, sayings, essays, interviews, etc. (alone or combined) to express interests, to focus on themes such as travel, to present issues such as drug use, homelessness, power, and identity, and to share information about services and surviving on the street.

The earlier version of the zine (*Slice*) started in the 1980s but ran into a series of censorship issues, and it was no longer supported by the safe house in which it was located (see Figure 2.5). While the center, funded by the provincial government, is reluctant to censor any contributions by the youth, they also draw the line at what they call "isms"—racism, sexism, etc.—or anything bordering on hate speech, which is a violation of the Canadian Charter of Rights.

Another Slice began in the late 1990s by one of the original *Slice* contributors—who also worked at the center while we were there—with the stated purpose of providing youth with "a venue for self-expression and freedom of thought" and was dedicated "to all young people coping with survival on the streets" (Ford, 2012). At the beginning of our project, hard copies of *Another Slice* were published several times a year, sometimes every month, including the themed issues (see Figure 2.6).

Later, a webzine in the form of a blog developed, as well as a site for uploaded back issues that were in a printed format. *Another Slice* expanded to include audio and video, as well as links to resources for youth in the city as discussed below (see www.anotherslice.ca). The webzine has journal-like entries, poetry, photographs, occasional uploaded handwritten writings, a page to remember youth who have died, and links to newspaper articles and Centre schedules, as well as separate links on the site to youth-created films and music.

As we noted in an earlier paper (Rogers and Winters, 2010), researchers have taken zines seriously in studies of popular youth culture, media studies, and to a lesser extent in literacy studies (Buckingham and Sefton-Green, 1994; Black and Steinkuehler, 2009; Guzzetti and Gamboa, 2004, Knobel and Lankshear, 2002). Fan magazines started in the 1930s are often seen as prototypes. Since then the zine format has been appropriated by a variety of "affinity groups" (Gee, 2004) such as 1960s political activists, punk rock musicians in the 1970s, and 1990s feminist and girl-power groups. More recently there has been a proliferation of countless groups

FIGURE 2.6 Sample cover from *Another Slice*

posting online zines (Rottmund, 2009; Knobel and Lankshear, 2002). Zines provide a space for these affinity groups to voluntarily come together to share information and participate in appropriating and transforming cultural materials to tell their own stories and build their own communities (Jenkins, 2006), and can be seen as a form of genre resistance in the sense of including historically excluded stories (Smith, 1993). From all these perspectives, it is argued that zines provide a rich perspective on the cultural production of youth in alternative communities.

Street zines, or homeless magazines, in particular, are part of a long and complex history of alternative newspapers and magazines in North America. The first street newspaper in North America may have been "Hobo News" from the 1910s and '20s in New York City, and there were an estimated fifty to seventy street or homeless newspapers and zines (Dodge, 1999). Street newspapers and zines often include poverty-related political issues and free expression with the intent of providing a platform for homeless people to regain independence and maintain self-respect. They include investigative journalism for social action, information for homeless, poetry and other literary writing, letters, photos, and essays, and often invoke traditional media discourses on the homeless and use sarcasm and irony, and the intended audiences are primarily local (Dodge, 1999; Torck, 2001).

A Slice of Youth Street Culture

Street culture is itself complex and multifaceted. At any given zine meeting, there might be self-identified "tweekers" (alternatively spelled "tweakers" and referring to drug users or former users), "train hoppers" (youth who travel on the trains), "twinkies" (those newer to the streets), youth from multigenerational families of "vagabonds," artists, poets, activists, and so on. Most street youth in Canada are designated as White/European-Canadian descent, about one-third as First Nations, and 4 percent as Black/African descent (2006; Public Health Agency of Canada); however, they represent a more complex range of ethnic and gender identifications and sexual orientations.

Some of the youth in this program had the equivalent of a secondary school education and others did not. Some were still on the streets and others were temporarily housed or couch surfing. That is, rather than a homogenous street youth culture, the group was made up of individuals and intersecting subgroups, each constructing particular fusions of identity positions or subjectivities based on their local situations, ethnicities, gender identities, interests/beliefs, projects, and goals. Sometimes these differences caused tensions in the larger group, and at other times they coalesced.

Homelessness itself was seen less as a fixed identity marker among the youth than as a temporary situation and affiliation. As one youth wrote: "It's nice when you can remind yourself that you're only living your life like this temporarily as a cautionary tale for your future self." Though many found it to be dangerous and difficult to live on the streets, they often expressed positive aspects of street life and culture—such as freedom, nonconformity, and a sense of community. One youth, Marcin, explained it this way in an interview conducted for a themed issue of the zine for a social worker audience:

> The thing is a lot of people on the street who choose to be on the street and constantly they're being bombarded with statements that they are doing something wrong—that they need help or need to change. "You're a victim of circumstance." Well no I'm not. The term homeless implies something missing. I call it "homefree." . . . I'm street man. I'm old school. I don't choose this forever. I don't know what the future holds. I'm not committed, but at the present time I don't appreciate being pushed for change all the time.

Because street youth often have tenuous and mobile subjectivities and affiliations, *Another Slice* served as a particularly unique space, though engagements with it were often fragile and incomplete, not unlike the literacy practices of marginalized youth in school contexts (Rogers and Schofield, 2005; Schofield and Rogers, 2004). Nonetheless they provide a powerful example of the sophisticated cultural productions youth are engaged in across diverse community contexts.

Entry into the Zine Program

Our initial entry into this program in the spring was fraught with concerns and unexpected responses. We were originally invited by the center manager to introduce computer literacy skills to the youth along with some equipment. However, the youth themselves were more cautious about our presence, and about the computers, and wanted to renegotiate our entry themselves. As the youth worker who ran the program at the time wrote in an email to us, "The youth [street youth in the zine program] are interested to know who you are and why you have chosen to fund our project." They expressed discomfort with conspicuous research practices, such as extensive note taking and filming, which is why we decided throughout our YouthCLAIM project to rely on jottings and to create our field notes away from the site. We did no videotaping at this site, though we occasionally sought permission to take photographs. In regard to the technologies that we eventually brought into the site (i.e., computers, cameras, printers), the youth were initially only interested in checking emails, taking photographs, and learning how to crop photos and store them on photo-sharing websites. They were also interested at the time in connecting to the *Homeless Nation* website.

In our role as participant-observers in this site, we provided disposable cameras and prints, computers, and printing of the zine for several issues as well as creative and technical support for writing and production. We began by observing the group for several weeks while they produced and published a paper version of the zine and created a homeless board game, "Bum Die," with clay (Figures 2.7–2.9).

The board game, a kind of street monopoly, included cards that read: *Someone stole your sleep spot, lose 5 bucks*; *Found $5.00 on the sidewalk*; *Spent all your money on a pair of used boots*; *Yuppy likes a punch line, score $200*; *Overdosed, go to jail*; *Mixed shrooms and skating, go to the hospital*; *Got busted*. The clay pieces for the board included a shopping cart, a hobo bag (sack on a stick), handcuffs, dog food, a three-legged dog, a backpack, a cup, and a squeegee. It was remarked that the game had no real goals or winners.

At these initial meetings, the youth were engaged in developing this board game, writing poetry on scraps of paper, and creating artwork, all in a handmade, DIY style. Much of this work focused on their own lives and desires—this was particularly apparent in conversations about the artwork and the board game.

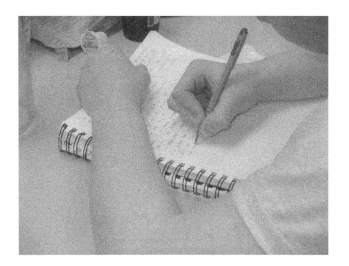

FIGURE 2.7 Youth writing at center

FIGURE 2.8 Youth working on Bum Die game

FIGURE 2.9 Clay pieces for Bum Die game

At one early meeting, a young woman working with pencil and paints explained her process to us (paraphrased from field-note jottings), which provides a sense of how they worked, including the play of embodied subjectivity that was often present in the conversations and work of the youth:

LU: I like to work in layers. I start my art with the furthest things away. Then I pencil on top. I sketch a pencil outline. Then I paint in the characters.

KARI-LYNN: Does the paint cover the pencil lines?

LU: If you use acrylics, then yes. As long as you don't add water. It's so nice to use straight acrylics. I haven't gotten to do that for a long time.

KARI-LYNN: Can you tell me about the painting itself?

LU: I like to use elements from people that I know. See, these are my shoes and those are my friend's jeans, and stuff. Nothing specifically. I don't want someone coming back and telling me I'm wrong.

KARI-LYNN: You know what I notice and like about your pictures? The women are not real skinny or anything.

LU: I draw the shape I aspire to be. I don't want to draw some skinny fuck like me.

Meetings also included impromptu conversations about what kinds of pieces might go in the zine and topics they might write about. During these discussions their facility with language play was also apparent. Dave, for instance, was planning to write about the center itself and its facilities and started to become quite negative about the various age restrictions and rules, to which Seth responded: "You've got cynical aftertaste."

When we returned in the autumn, there was a new youth worker for the zine program and we were invited to provide more informal teaching, and technical and material support for writing, photography, and zine production, which included photographs, artwork, word games, ads, posters, poetry, and other creative and hybrid literary and expository writings. For the writing workshops we chose to work with the youth in less structured and more spontaneous ways given the range of moods and dispositions we observed. Some youth were there mainly for the food and for the occasional monetary compensation for their contributions (e.g., five dollars for a zine page was sometimes available from the staff). Some were there for the social interaction. Others were more interested in creating the zine.

When students did write, they were often averse to prompts or revising their work. When an outside poet came in to create these approaches with a more standard workshop model with them we could see that it was met with much resistance. Our approach was to listen to their ongoing conversations and from there suggest writing ideas, sometimes including several youth. One evening several of the youth were talking about feeling tired and and that it was just another "shitty Sunday." Theresa wondered aloud if they might each share what a shitty Sunday feels, tastes, and smells like, which resulted in a group poem. Some youth preferred other forms of writing (e.g., letters, essays) or avoided writing as a medium. When Marcin had strong ideas about what kinds of things social workers need to know about homeless youth we suggested he write those ideas down but he refused because he didn't like to write. Theresa then suggested a taped interview that could be transcribed, to which he agreed and included a friend in the process. Other youth preferred visual modalities, such as drawing, painting, photography, creating posters, and creating a variety of hybrid visual and print texts.

In these autumn and early winter meetings, in their work, and on the zine pages, the youth continued to depict their lives, share their interests, or argue philosophically or politically about issues important to them, including drug use, trust, issues of power and identity, outreach services for homeless youth, and surviving on the street.

Homelessness Remixed

As we have noted, the youth engaged in playful and sophisticated uses of language, and multimodal and genre resources, as they produced these various kinds of texts. It became clear to us early on that their work exhibited a kind of flexibility with genres as dynamic cultural forms and social practices, described by theorists such as Bakhtin (1986) and Briggs and Bauman (1992), and more recently understood as "remix" culture (e.g., Knobel and Lankshear, 2011; Jocson, 2013). Their facility with genre play, in particular, provides a lens for examining the ways the youth juxtapose and transform literacy genres and forms across modalities in order to recognize and resist power structures (Buckingham and Sefton-Green, 1994; Stein, 2008; Lemke, 1995; Manovich, 2001).

Viewed as a form of autobiographical practice, the zine include a kind of "genre resistance" by using stories, forms, and positions that are typically historically excluded or marginalized (Smith, 1993). The "constructedness" of zines is seen to be particularly noteworthy—the way the zines call attention to their own process through the "presentation of the text and images, layout, and photocopying quality, and how they effect, interact with, contradict, or interrupt the narrative" (Poletti, 2008, p. 88).

The youth often used hybrid genres and forms while also using print literacies layered with multimodal literacies for particular critical effect. Below are two examples. In Figure 2.10, the youth has used an already hybridized form—a visual puzzle—that asks the viewer to locate used needles ("rigs") in the Downtown Eastside of the city—an area well-known for poverty, drug use, sex workers, and crime as well as for community activism.

As was illustrated in the opening vignette about Jordan, the disposal of rigs is a particular issue for street youth, who often pick up part-time work through the center cleaning up used needles. Though many of the youth are drug users or former users themselves, they resent those who carelessly dispose of needles in public places, including schoolyards and parks where children are put at risk, when there are needle disposal boxes available, as is represented in the puzzle. The effect here is to provide immediate engagement by the viewer into the problem without proselytizing, but rather with the more sophisticated approach of using an ironic tone ("Long Live Hastings") that makes reference to the street that is most

FIGURE 2.10 Visual puzzle from paper version of zine

well-known for drug-related activities. The use of "Long Live . . ." may reference issues of continuity of "power" or in this case, a kind of powerlessness to address a social issue. The mix of visuals and text throughout signal meaningful cultural references (graffiti, trash, a stairwell, etc.) to the destitution along a street that they avoid and often see as a kind of warning sign—a life many clearly say they do not want to emulate as adults.

Jae, in her poem "Yuppy Muck" (below), draws on the combination of a traditional poetic form and irony to address cultural discourses about urban homelessness.

Yuppy Muck

Tripping time to waste away
Broken souls rot to decay
Cityscapes the goal [goat] of me
Fringed with lies and vanity

You bastards walk with noses high
Lamb skin coats, no wonder why
A travesty mole on your city face
"Souls of the Street are such a disgrace"

We are proof this city's fucked
Chill for a while, now we're stuck
Watch the needles shoot the drug
Another problem swept under the rug

Know this in heart you sorry fuck
My feet are trapped in your city muck
You don't care, think your [sic] so wise
You who cause your cities [sic] demise

While Jae has chosen here to use one of the most traditional print genres—a ballad-like poem with four line stanzas (quatrains) with a consistent meter and rhymed couplets, the statement is fresh and confrontational. Jae exploits the contrasting stereotypical discourses defining "yuppies" and "homeless" for her own purpose. Yuppies are "time-wasting," have "broken souls," and are narcissistic liars "fringed with lies and vanity." Street people are drug addicts (shooting up) and are ruining the city—are a "disgrace." At the same time the poem is held together by the idea that street people are simply the scapegoats for a host of societal ills—that blame is in fact misplaced in the discourses about "problems" the city faces.

In a page from the tattoo issue (Figure 2.11) from the online version of the webzine Jae again uses a traditional poetic form, this time with a play of images and text.

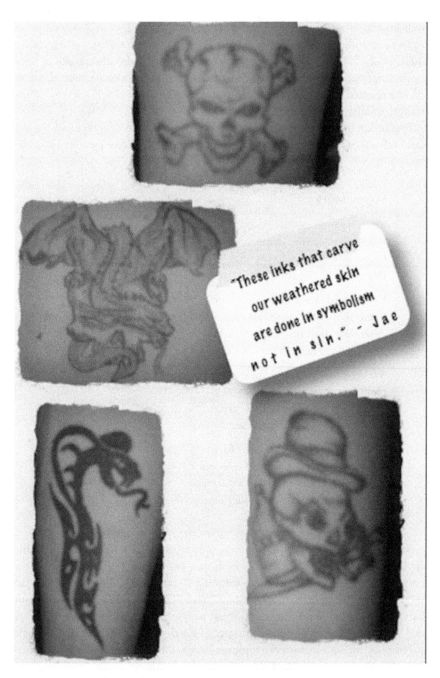

FIGURE 2.11 Page from online tattoo issue

This page has photographs of actual tattoos of participating youth overlaid with an original poem by Jae that is written this time in classical rhyming couplets: "These inks that carve/our weathered skin/are done in symbolism/not in sin." The poem provides a clear and simple yet highly eloquent statement of resistance to being stereotyped by choosing to inscribe their identities on their bodies. These pages from the zine examples are among many that incorporate multimodal textual play as cultural critique—through combinations, layerings, and juxtapsoitions of genres, forms, and modalities.

Countering Homelessness: Repositioning Youth on the Street

The street youth at this center were drawing on their embodied subjectivities, together with linguistic and semiotic tools of irony (as illustrated in the visual puzzle and poetry above) and parody to position themselves and critique larger cultural discourses and practices. These tools also included the tactical poaching of cultural material, as parody often does. The poem below (Figure 2.12) is a particularly clear example of the way the youth readily parody and transform popular culture and media forms. Here the familiar credit card advertisement that, in its orignal form, concisely commodifies presumably middle class family relationships

FIGURE 2.12 Parody of a common advertisement

is appropriated by Jae effectively make a counter-narrative statement about homelessness.

The slogan in Figure 2.12 reads: "Slice of Pizza—$1/ Pack of Smokes—$7/ Bag of Weed—$25/ Your own place to live away from the streets/ FUCKING PRICELESS." The person visually represented in this remixed ad is sitting on a street with trademark Doc Martens-style boots popular among street youth. Though this originally filmed ad is a common target of parody (there are many textual versions online, including sites that invite people to make their own "priceless" MasterCard commercial), Jae's version is original—pointedly contrasting the gulf between those who live on the margins of society and the assumed audience of the original ad.

Nonetheless, she laments her "lack of originality" and use of a "marketing ploy," a kind of self-critique that adds another layer of literate commentary and awareness. In case the meaning was not fully grasped by less sophisticated readers, a clearer version is appended—noting that everyone wants a home. This zine page repositions Jae as someone who "speaks back to power" with humor (parody), awareness, insight, and a clear counter narrative. We found that these linguistic tools of parody and irony were often incorporated into the zine pages, along with a playfulness with text forms, resulting in clear and powerful messages that ran counter to common discourses about street youth. Popular cultural imagery in zines is used to resist these dominant discourses, closing "the gap between media and consumer, allowing individual zinesters to reuse the language of the dominant public spheres of discourse to situate their life writing" (Poletti, 2005, p. 189).

While many of the youth we worked with in the zine project had a range of conventional literacy skills—some more limited—they had many tactics and resources to convey their messages and often did, sometimes with our support or the support of other youth workers, as in the case of Jordan in the opening vignette. In declaring that people on the street do more than drugs all day, and by illustrating his own concerns about drug use through his zine page, he is consciously producing discourses that run counter to the way the youth were being constructed by others both in media and through lived experiences and interactions with people on the streets. Looking back at all of the examples above it is clear that by appropriating traditional discourses, hybridizing genres and forms, and using parody or irony, the youth were talking back to or disrupting "repetitive citations" (Davies, 2008) about street youth that disempowered them, and thereby repositioned themselves in relation to their audiences. Their repositionings were complex and often improvisational; sometimes they distanced themselves from or rejected homelessness, sometimes they embraced it, and at other times they remixed the larger discourses that positioned and constrained them. These counter narratives served to resist and challenge the legitimacy of the original discourses, thus creating a strong cultural critique and public claims.

A poem by Fraggle provides another clear example of a counter narrative that presupposes an awareness of and struggle against the lenses through which street youth are viewed, a poem that was eventually reprinted in the poetry chapbook (Mills and Rogers, 2009.) that was launched in public community center (see Figure 2.13).

FIGURE 2.13 Cover of poetry anthology

FIGURE 2.13 (Continued)

The Truth (hurts)

by Fraggle Rawk (2009)

This one is for you
you with the starbucks 100 dollar haircut
you there, the one with mcmurder double cheeseburger super happiness
the one on the cell phone that drives 100,000 dead iraqi mobile
to all the girls with something to prove, mini skirt madness on
granville street

to all the pretentious hippie cats that think smoking pot will solve the
worlds problems
to all you douchebags, the roxy-roofie-colada-wet-dream-hair-gel types
the ones who listen to britney spears, lindsay lohan and think they piss
perfume
the suits with expensive ties that could feed an African family for a year
i know you probably dont hear me
im not sure that i speak your language
i know you probably cant see me
money seems to make one conspicuous enough to acknowledge
now please, before you spit on me, study me or sweep me underneath
your carpet that stretches on like the sea
sit on this concrete
tell me how it feels
sleep under these stars
tell me how you sleep
if we strip away the layers
that make you who you think you are
what is left for you?
if we take away your cell phone
who is talking now?
If it were all to come crashing down
who will be the one left shivering in the cold?

I've come to find myself quite comfortable under this
carpet below the poverty line
my comfort is in the knowledge of the life that i know is real
for life isn't cocktail parties and orgy's in oil
when it all comes crashing down
i will be the one to take your hand
tell you that there is life beyond your line of credit
money can't save your soul
the truth shall set you free
but then again
you can't hear me

Here Fraggle turns the discourses of yuppie/poverty on its head. *Yuppies* is
generally the term street youth use for all middle and upper-class co-dwellers of
the city. In the poem, the habits of yuppies are clearly critiqued and seen as pretentious, vacuous, and conspicuous, while street youth as embodied by this narrator
are poor, invisible, and unheard. Yet, at the same time the poem is held together by
the idea that street people are in fact stronger, freer, and more real, yet ultimately
no different; her warning to yuppies is a powerful counter narrative to what the

youth are subjected to on the streets and in the media—that they are a lazy and a blight on the city. Other youth in the collection created similar counter narratives that back to the "rich man," CEOs, the stigmatizations of homeless youth, as well as narratives directed to the indigenous community describing a ceremony on unceded lands that honors traditions and teachings.

Homelessness 101: Taking it Back to the Streets

Over time, the zine also moved from a more local to a potentially global audience by moving to the online webzine format. The idea of moving the zine to an online site was initially met with resistance. Originally it was connected to *Homeless Nation*; however, several of the youth in the zine group felt that too many "yuppies" were voyeurs on that site. During a meeting toward the end of our project, the youth were arguing about who could have access for uploading materials to the new website created just for the zine. Eli suggested that anyone who came to the *Another Slice* meetings should have access, but Lu responded that "by allowing anyone to have uploading access, the site might become too yuppified like *Homeless Nation* and not their own anymore." A sense of ownership and control that the DIY paper zine fostered seemed to be in doubt with this new platform.

This conversation reflects issues taken up in scholarly communities related to the problem of researchers and others acting as online lurkers and related issues of privacy and trust. It is evident that the street youth engaged in various online communities to maintain relationships and connections (Leander and McKim, 2003) but were clearly aware that various groups might be using their sites for purposes other than what they were intended for and so remained wary of such practices.

The youth were also concerned that moving the zine online would cause it to lose "its soul" as a street newspaper. It is interesting to note that though the very "soul" of the zine—the street newspaper aspect—was in fact a literacy practice that originally traveled from more distant sites historically and geographically, though locally situated, and is in effect now traveling outward again in a new form. As the group shifted to newer and younger participants there was less and less resistance and more positive reactions to the idea of having comments and feedback on their work. According to the arts program director, although the webzine is now fully online (www.anotherslice.ca), it still has a "do-it-yourself" culture in that all aspects are still under the control of the youth. Youth are welcome to scan any of their work and the director will upload it for them to keep the DIY feel and look. He also prints copies for youth by request. The website is now linked to a Facebook page and to Twitter. In addition, postcards are produced that can be handed out on the street to direct people to the site (see Figure 2.14).

The move from off-line paper version to a more fluid on- and off-line space brought into relief issues of audience that had intrigued us from the beginning of our work at this site. It was ideal for us, as researchers, to witness and participate in the off-line iteration of the zine as it gave us a deeper understanding of the DIY

Another Slice is an online zine created by and about the lives of street youth. Contact us online or through our home at Directions Youth Services Center. 1134 Burrard street Vancouver , BC. V6z 1y7 604 633-1472 WWW.anotherslice.ca

FIGURE 2.14 Postcard for *Another Slice*

processes behind the development of the online presence. Many youth seemed to be mainly concerned with reaching a local audience, and were content to hand out copies locally to friends, social workers, or strangers on the streets, sometimes in exchange for money for themselves or to support the production of new issues. However, others were quite interested in a broader audience.

This deep connection to the local, along with a fascination with the responses they receive online with hundreds of hits per month, speaks to questions of youth arts, media, and literacy and public engagement. As mentioned above, the webzine includes the "Slice Blog," music podcasts, and links, including to a Facebook page that also links to all of the archived paper zines that were published over the course of twenty years, from 1992 to 2012 (*Slice* and *Another Slice* versions).

We theorize our work with the street youth, and with youth in all of the sites in this project, as a kind of public pedagogy in which learning takes place, as Giroux (2003) and others describe it, in a range of public spheres, from small to larger publics. This public pedagogical frame allows us to examine the intersection of the claims of youth as public bodies in particular spaces with the larger challenges of democracy and social justice in a "newly constituted global public" (Giroux, 2003, p. 9), and the potential to link these struggles to classrooms and other educational spaces. This work asks us to see learning spaces as "ambiguous spaces of cultural address" (Sandlin, Schultz, and Burdick, 2010, p. 3) that allow us to imagine extending educational acknowledgement and support to youth who are engaging with literacy, arts, and media to make public claims about social injustice.

In fact, it could be argued that the creators of *Another Slice* are, in many ways, more engaged in public life than many middle class, housed adolescents who attend schools every day. In addition to actively producing public counter narratives in virtually every issue, they created a special issue of their zine that addressed those becoming social workers (Mills, 2008). In the inside front cover, it reads:

> This edition of Another Slice is an outlet for street entrenched youth to share their thoughts and feelings about the system created to serve them; a system that is often less than ideal. We hope that social work students can learn from these words. We hope you take them to heart.

In this issue there are poems about homelessness, stories of inadequate counseling, interviews that talk about the problem of attempting to change rather than support street youth and the danger of shelters, and essays by youth suffering from addiction and mental illness about the "school of the streets." At the end of one section of a printed interview between Theresa and two youth (described above), Marcin and Slynkee, titled *Talkin: A dialogue about street youth, social workers, and the Charter of Rights*, Marcin shifts from speaking about to directly addressing social workers:

MARCIN: I'm street man. I'm old school. I don't choose this forever. I don't know what the future holds. I'm not committed, but at the present time I don't appreciate being pushed for change all the time. I think that's why social workers burn out—because they are trying to change you and you don't want to change. It can be deceiving. You ask for something and they turn you away because you are not suffering. But if you play the victim role, "I'm cold, I need help," and this and that then you get help. It's not fair you're in the same situation as everyone else. Do I need to play victim role to get it? Social workers need to look at that. Where's the equality in that? . . . It's demoralizing if you play the sympathy game for too long. They take our choices away from us. They don't let you live the way we want to live. They say we are doing something wrong and restricting us—like if you don't sleep inside, you can't sleep anywhere and they take away our rights Why not sleep in Stanley Park? A cop on a horse will beat the crap out of you. They tell you it's not for sleeping. They say the park is not for sleeping. But you can only be on the sidewalk if you're in motion and have a place to go. Do you know technically it is illegal to ask someone what time it is? It is illegal to solicit anyone for money, service or property. Like panhandling—if you ask someone for something you get a fine with a deadline.

SLYNKEE: I look at my debts as my high score in the video game of life.

MARCIN: If you don't pay it you get a warrant for your arrest. They're lax on that but it's gonna change—the Olympics are coming. Pretty much you've gotta protect your rights. And social workers should keep that in mind when they deal with homeless, street people, drug addicts and I think they should be there to defend people's rights. *Don't treat them like victims—they are aware of their choices or you can make them aware of their choices—inform them of their choices. There are some who are victims of circumstances but not everyone is like that. If you bombard them with that you make them victims* [italics added].

These direct addresses to the public were evident other ways as well. Many of the youth also engaged in various forms of public critique beyond the zine or the project itself. Some were involved in a local youth theatre project unpacking as a form of resistance to the closure of safe houses (Wager, 2014). Others participated in radio interviews/podcasts about homelessness in the city. Still others contributed to *Homeless Nation*, a national social network website created by and for the street community.

Street youth sometimes attended public community dialogues, conducted interviews in the press and on the radio, and participated in center events with the city mayor, the governor-general, and other political leaders. Once a year several youth perform music and spoken-word poetry at a downtown café where they also display paper anniversary issues of the zine, usually to a full house. In these ways, the youth became more visible and, in a sense, created new publics (Hickey-Moody, 2013) for their claims.

Another form of public engagement is evident in a follow-up project at the center, titled "Another Slice University," in which we collaborated with the Media Programs Facilitator, Colin, to support youth films that educate academics and the larger public about homelessness. The films were posted on iTunes University and also shown at a downtown film festival (see http://anotherslice.ca/main/video for a link to the iTunes site).

The films were focused on countering the misguided assumptions that the public make about homeless people, on how youth end up on the street, on how homeless people are treated when trying to find work, and on issues related to programming for street youth. For one film, we worked with a young man named Steven, showing him how he might develop a storyboard for a video idea about the issue of triggers in the Downtown Eastside (DTES). Figures 2.15, 2.16, and 2.17 show notes and drawings from the storyboard phase and a clip from the film itself, which is titled with the words "A relapse trigger is any person, place, thing or situation which reminds the person of the drug or alcohol use." Within the part of town that young man walks in the film, in the DTES, there are many free services provided for the homeless, but the area is also known for its drug visibility and accessibility. As Steven points out, this presents a daily dilemma for many street-entrenched youth because entering this part of town can easily trigger their addictions. He decided he wanted to take the viewer on a walk from the side of town where he accessed youth services he preferred to the DTES. Although Steven left Vancouver before it was finished, other youth and Colin finished filming and editing the video.

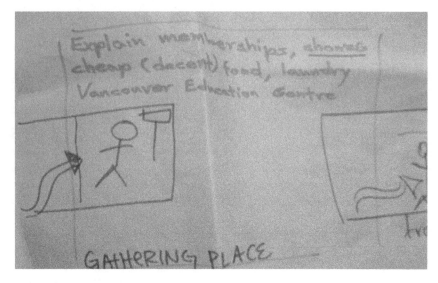

FIGURE 2.15 Storyboard notes for Steven's film

FIGURE 2.16 Sketches for storyboard for Steven's film

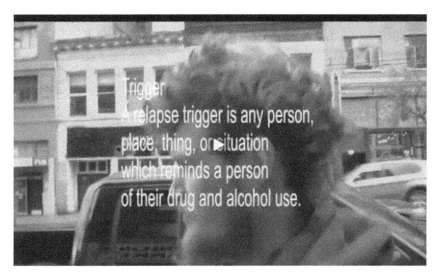

FIGURE 2.17 Shot from Steven's film

Steven's film, titled *Triggers*, links to other civic engagement activities he participated in, such as presenting to a local foundation about homelessness to over a
hundred people. In an interview (see Rogers, Schroeter, Wager, and Hauge, 2014),
he recalls speaking at the forum, where he pointed out some of the limitations of
centers that serve street-entrenched youth. He ends his comments with a strong
address to a public audience, expressing his frustration that they do not understand
the importance of people, of staff, in serving homeless youth. Here, Steven demands
legibility and recognizability as he attempts to relocate responsibility for understanding a particular social policy issue on his audience, the larger public:

STEVEN: I said that, uh, you know, all the centers are good, it's just that there are
certain quirks about them that throw them off. Like [this one] I can't access
now that I'm twenty-two, I can still come in for *Another Slice* and I can go
to [the work program] until I'm twenty-four, but I can't come in for meals
unless I'm fucking starving and then I can only come in once a week at that.
Um, you know, just stuff like that and I explained that, uh, sure, you know,
you could give us a bunch of money and fuck everything up and make a new
center, but in the staff, in the long run it's all gonna end up coming down to
the staff. You could lose all the staff that you have in these centers and hire
new staff to run a new center, and if the staff is no good, nobody's gonna use
the new center and you've just fucking wasted everything that we've had.

THERESA: It's all about the staff.

STEVEN: Yeah. And it's funny 'cause, like, everybody, that was like a real "ding!"
for like the whole fucking room.

THERESA: Really?

STEVEN: Yeah, it kind of blew my mind. It was like, are you people fucking retarded?

From the beginning of work at the center to the end, we witnessed the range of ways the youth "took it back to the streets"—sharing their work and their views with small and large, local and broader public audiences. Very early in our work we brainstormed with one arts volunteer about making the youth work more public, and creating and supporting what we considered a form of public pedagogy:

ARTS VOLUNTEER: Maybe the issue is that nobody speaks up for them. You can do a show, and if it's just the same people that can come . . .

THERESA: Maybe inviting people widen their audience . . . where does their voice go?

ARTS VOLUNTEER: If we got as far as doing film, I know some people who could pay them to do acting and stuff . . . I know some community film makers who might be able to connect with them . . . doors to open, ways to let them in. The film world is transient, always moving, on to the next project, so that might be a suitable lifestyle . . . It's about community building within their own community . . .

KARI-LYNN: Maybe we can find a way to talk to the city to give space for graffiti? As people from the university maybe we can write a letter and get some public space. That's what we did with [another program for youth]. All they did was contact the city. Maybe somewhere at the university?

ARTS WORKER: Or would they like to have an exhibition up at the university?

THERESA: Another space is in the Education cafeteria. If the artwork is framed or whatever. All the teacher education students would see it—it would be great to also do an event where they talk directly to folks . . . We could also do photography. I can get access to digital cameras that they would use. We could give them disposable cameras. We could have computers too that they can use. Slide shows can be made in a three-hour workshop.

In the end, we did provide cameras and computers, printed copies of the zines, helped to organize a gallery event at their downtown space, created a poetry chapbook, and later uploaded the *Homeless 101* films on a university iTunes site. The zine and other art projects became a webzine. There were public viewings and performances of the artwork, zines, and music at the center, and a film festival at a public theatre downtown with an audience of over one hundred people. We continue to share the youth zines and films with our teacher education students. The youth themselves participate in a variety of public events and speak out in newspapers, conferences, on the radio, and other public forums.

The public pedagogy framework reflected here speaks to both the local, mobile, and tenuous affiliations of the street youth community, and their broader social and political awareness and concerns and their active engagement in participatory culture (Jenkins et al., 2009)—that is, as producers of culture in a connected community. The advent and availability of new media and digital technologies can support youth who engage in participatory culture through literacy production, particularly through online and Web 2.0 platforms. Even in the paper version of the zine, the street youth had ready access to popular culture and media that enabled them to appropriate discursive resources, use multiple, layered modalities (old and new), and borrow and hybridized genres. They effortlessly moved toward irony and parody (Buckingham and Sefton-Green, 1994) as counter-narrative pedagogies (Kellner and Share, 2005) and, in turn, as a form of engaged citizenship (Boler, 2008). The connected space of the online platform provides a more immediate sharing of their work and ideas with a broader audience without necessarily sacrificing the DIY aspect, though it did lessen our access to the various ways they worked, and does not replace the face-to-face and local connections the youth maintain.

The work of the youth speaks to and reaches a range of publics and counter-publics (Fraser, 1993; Warner, 2002) that include alternative or little publics (Hickey-Moody, 2013) that form a kind of aesthetic citizenship in civic spaces where youth voices are heard through performance or the materiality of art. We might also consider these youth voices as "shouts on the street" (Stewart, 1983)—moments in which youth subjectivity was constituted through complex discursive participation in civic life—drawing on the resources of their embodied lives, arts, media, and literacy to engage and resist larger societal and cultural discourses as they sought to make themselves more legible and recognizable public citizens.

In our closing chapter we further theorize the relationship between the work of the youth in this site, as well as the anti-violence and theatre performance sites, and the implications for understanding the relationship of arts, media, and critical literacy practices among youth, public pedagogy, and the intersections of local and global participation in democratic citizenship.

Notes

1 The center, open twenty-four hours a day and seven days a week, seeks to provide Vancouver's homeless youth access to the tools, support, and guidance they need to make positive changes in their lives. The center works closely with the community to develop solutions to end youth homelessness in Vancouver and to change the community's perception of street-involved youth.

2 Though Jordan had low literacy skills, struggling with print didn't appear to be a common problem in this community. Throughout our time working in this zine program, we found that several street entrenched youth were adept readers and writers. Some of their

favorite authors included Shakespeare, Michael Slade, Jean Paul Sartre, Stephen King, and John Grisham.
3 We found out in a later interview that Jordan completed grade 8, but that he struggles with literacy. He wrote: "I'm still learning to read and write. My girlfriend is teaching me. I'd like to write stories but I've never been good at it. I made it to grade 8 in Ontario. I've always done artwork . . ."
4 The original zine had been discontinued because of content that was deemed to be bordering on "hate speech" toward certain groups. When *Another Slice* was restarted in 2006, a poster outlining the "rules of conduct" for the youth services center was referred to as a guideline. The rules included the statement "No racist, derogatory, homophobic remarks or comments."

References

Bakhtin, M. M. (1986). *Speech genres and other late essays*. Austin: University of Texas Press.
Black, R. W., & Steinkuehler, C. (2009). Literacy in virtual worlds. In L. Christenbury, R. Bomer, & P. Smagorinsky (Eds.), *Handbook of adolescent literacy research* (pp. 271–286). New York: Guilford.
Boler, M. (2008). *Digital media and democracy*. Toronto: University of Toronto Press.
Briggs, C., & Bauman, R. (1992). Genre, intertextuality and social power. *Journal of Linguistic Anthropology, 2*(2), 131–172.
Buckingham, D., & Sefton-Green, J. (1994). *Cultural studies goes to school*. Bristol: Taylor & Francis.
Davies, B. (2008). Re-thinking "behavior" in terms of positioning and the ethics of responsibility. In A. M. Phelan & J. Sumsion (Eds.), *Provoking absences: Critical readings in teacher education* (pp. 173–186). Rotterdam, Netherlands: Sense Publishers.
Dodge, C. (1999). Words on the street: Homeless people's newspapers. *American Libraries, 30*(7), 60–62.
Ford, C. (2012). Letter from the Editor. In *Another Slice: 20th Anniversary Edition*. Retrieved September 4, 2013, from www.anotherslice.ca
Fraser, N. (1993). Rethinking the public sphere: A contribution to the critique of actually existing democracy. In S. During (Ed.), *The cultural studies reader* (pp. 518–536). New York: Routledge.
Gee, J. P. (2004). *Situated language and learning: A critique of traditional schooling*. New York: Routledge.
Giroux, H. (2003). Public pedagogy and the politics of resistance: Notes on a critical theory of educational struggle. *Educational Philosophy and Theory, 35*(1), 5–16.
Guzzetti, B., & Gamboa, M. (2004). Zines for social justice: Adolescent girls writing on their own. *Reading Research Quarterly, 39*(4), 408–436.
Hickey-Moody, A. (2013). *Youth, arts and education: Reassembling subjectivity through affect*. New York: Routledge.
Jenkins, H. (2006). *Convergence culture: Where old and new media collide*. New York: NYU Press.
Jenkins, H., Clinton, K., Purushotma, R., Robison, A. J., & Weigel, M. (2009). *Confronting the challenges of participatory culture: Media education for the 21st century*. Cambridge, MA: MIT Press.
Jocson, K. M. (2013). Remix revisited: Critical solidarity in youth media arts. *E–Learning and Digital Media, 10*(1), 68–82.

Kellner, D., & Share, J. (2005). Toward critical media literacy: Core concepts, debates, organizations, and policy. *Discourse: Studies in the Cultural Politics of Education, 26*(3), 369–386.

Knobel, M., & Lankshear, C. (2002). Cut, paste, publish: The production and consumption of zines. In D. Alvermann (Ed.), *Adolescents and literacies in a digital world* (pp. 164–185). New York: Peter Lang.

Knobel, M., & Lankshear, C. (2011). Remix: The art and craft of endless hybridization. *Journal of Adolescent & Adult Literacy, 52*(1), 22–33.

Leander, K. M., & McKim, K. (2003). Tracing the everyday "sitings" of adolescents on the Internet: A strategic adaptation of ethnography across online and offline spaces. *Education, Communication and Information, 3*(2), 211–240.

Lemke, J. (1995). *Textual politics.* London: Taylor and Francis.

Manovich, L. (2001). *The language of new media.* Cambridge, MA: MIT Press.

Mills, E. (Ed.). (2008). *Another slice: By youth 4 social workers.* Retrieved from www.anotherslice.ca

Mills, E., & Rogers, T. (Eds.). (2009). *Words from the street: Writings from* Another Slice. Vancouver: SPN Publishing.

Poletti, A. (2005). Self-publishing in the global and local: Situating life writing in zines. *Biography, 28*(1), 183–192.

Poletti, A. (2008). Auto/assemblage: Reading the zine. *Biography,* 31(1), 85–102.

Public Health Agency of Canada (2006). Street youth in Canada. Available at www.publichealth.gc.ca/sti. Accessed 18 October 2014.

Rachlis, B. S., Wood, E., Zhang, R., Montaner, J. S., & Kerr, T. (2009). High rates of homelessness among a cohort of street-involved youth. *Health & Place, 15*(1), 10–17.

Rawk, F. (2009). The truth (hurts). In E. Mills & T. Rogers (Eds.), *Words from the street: Writings from* Another Slice. Vancouver: SPN Publishing.

Rogers, T., & Schofield, A. (2005). Things thicker than words: Portraits of youth multiple literacies in an alternative secondary program. In J. Anderson, M. Kendrick, T. Rogers, & S. Smythe (Eds.), *Portraits of literacy across families, communities and schools* (pp. 205–220). Mahwah, NJ: Lawrence Erlbaum Associates.

Rogers, T., Schroeter, S., Wager, A., & Hauge, C. (2014). Public pedagogies of street-entrenched youth: New literacies, identity and social critique. In K. Sanford, T. Rogers, & M. Kendrick (Eds.), *Everyday youth literacies: Critical perspectives for new times* (pp. 47–61). Singapore: Springer Publications.

Rogers, T., & Winters, K. (2010). Textual play, satire, and counter discourses of street youth 'zining practices. In D. Alvesmann (Ed.), *Adolescents' online literacies: Connecting classrooms, digital media, and popular culture* (pp. 91–108). New York: Peter Lang.

Rottmund, K. (2009). A little bit about everything you need to know about zines. *Visual Literacy.* Retrieved from http://aclayouthservices.pbworks.com/Visual-Literacy

Sandlin, J., Schultz, B. D., & Burdick, J. (Eds.). (2010). *Handbook of public pedagogy.* New York: Routledge

Schofield, A., & Rogers, T. (2004). At play in fields of ideas: Teaching curriculum and the lives of youth. *Journal of Adolescent and Adult Literacies, 48,* 238–248.

Smith, S. (1993). Who's talking/who's talking back? The subject of personal narrative. *Signs, 18*(2), 392–407.

Sontag, S. (1999). *Posters, advertisement, art, political artifact, commodity.* In M. Bierut, S. Helfand, S. Heller, & R. Poyner (Eds.), *Looking closer 3: Classic writings on graphic design* (pp. 196–218). New York: Allworth Press.

Stein, P. (2008). Multimodal instructional practices. In J. Coiro, M. Knobel, C. Lankshear, & D. Leu (Eds.), *Handbook of research on new literacies* (pp. 1–22). New York: Lawrence Erlbaum Associates.

Stewart, S. (1983). Shouts on the street: Bakhtin's anti-linguistics. *Critical Inquiry, 10,* 265–281.

Torck, D. (2001). Voices of homeless people in street newspapers: A cross-cultural exploration. *Discourse and Society, 12*(3), 371–392.

Wager, A. C. (2014). *Learning out of the ordinary: Applied theatre as pedagogy with street youth* (PhD diss.). University of British Columbia, Vancouver.

Warner, M. (2002). Publics and counterpublics. *Public Culture, 14*(1), 49–90.

Winters, K. (2010). Quilts of authorship: A literature review of multimodal assemblage in the field of literacy education. *Canadian Journal for New Scholars in Education, 3*(1), 1–12.

3

LEAVING OUT VIOLENCE

Talking Back to the Community through Film

I shoved a pin through my face. My mom hates it, but you know, it's rad.
Kaity, in the LOVE program, talking about her self-pierced lips

A group of about fifteen youth voluntarily participated in a video production workshop in the large back room of an Eastside youth community center as part of LOVE, an anti-violence program with sites in five cities in North America.[1] The youth ranged between fifteen and twenty years old and came to the video project in the evenings. Many of the youth had contributed writings, photography, and poetry to the LOVE newspaper, *ONE L.O.V.E.*, via a photojournalism workshop; however, prior to this new workshop they had not made their own videos in the program (see Figures 3.1 and 3.2).

The twelve youth are dressed in comfortable clothes, mostly jeans and sweatshirts; some have pink, purple, or green hair or dreadlocks or face piercings, while others appear more conventionally dressed. Students are White, South-Asian Canadian and African-Canadian. Anne-Marie, who is leading a video workshop that takes place partway through the year we worked with the group, introduces filmic elements and brings up the topic of youth stereotypes. "What are the stereotypes of youth we see in society and popular media?" she asks. The group throws out words like "hoodlums" and "thugs." Erin responds that many youth are seen as "criminals" because of the clothes they wear—like black hoodies. Kaity notes that you can tell the difference between grunge kids and yuppie kids by their clothes.

Anne-Marie then shows excerpts from a film called *Reel Bad Arabs: How Hollywood Vilifies a People* to extend the conversation to stereotyping in Hollywood films. She asks "why do you think Hollywood would want to profile Arabs this way?" Max, a tall African-Canadian young man with long dreadlocks, is less

FIGURE 3.1 Framed photo by youth hanging at the community center

FIGURE 3.2 Framed photo by youth hanging at the community center

interested in talking about Arabs and moves the conversation to the stereotyping of African-Americans by pointing out that they are mostly stereotyped in movies—as criminals, as overly sexualized, as thieves, or as gang members. He goes on, "but everyone is seen in one way or another in movies and even in life unless you get to know them." Kaity says that the Arabs are made to look like "nasty" people—"it's easy to see how people might judge them based on the way Hollywood portrays them." Nichelle comments that Hollywood does that to make money—that these [stereotypic] portrayals are entertaining.

Anne-Marie then shows a short video previously made by two of the youth (Erin and Jenn) called *Sheepin* to demonstrate the intuitive use of "stereotyped" images. The film begins with a photo of a crowded school hallway overlaid with the words "Pay Attention; How are we the same?" We then see alternating images of sheep and students played to the Pink Floyd song, "We don't need no education." Anne-Marie asked what they thought of the photo of the teacher (see Figures 3.3 and 3.4).

FIGURE 3.3 Image of sheepdog from *Sheepin* film

FIGURE 3.4 Image of teacher from *Sheepin* film

They say that she just looked like a teacher, with, as one youth points out, that "ugly-ass pea-green turtleneck sweater." Anne-Marie suggests that stereotypes work in movies because they are a visual shorthand that rapidly sends a message to the audience. The conversation then turns to the idea of reversing stereotypes to make the point that they distort our understanding of a group of people. Reversing a stereotype, making portrayals funny by exaggerating them, creates a parody, which the youth point out is a way to criticize the way they are judged. The group decides to make a film about youth stereotypes. Anne-Marie suggests they download some images from the Internet to create a storyboard, similar to what they had done earlier in our project for their "identity" films, but they prefer to just begin filming various ideas themselves. They film for the rest of the workshop and then edit their movie the following week.

The result is a film called *Teenage Kicks* (see http://theresarogers.ca/youthclaim) that features Max enacting a somewhat obscene gesture to indicate his perceived sexuality; an Indo-Canadian boy portraying a drug user, saying "I pop two tabs of acid, two caps of E and you're done—you're good for the night"; a White girl acting like a very quiet and shy "emo," saying in a very quiet and slow voice, "People call me emo but I'm not really. Just because I write poetry . . . and a blog . . . doesn't mean I'm emo. Sure, I wear mascara, but so do the other girls"; and closing with someone in the background asking about piercings and Kaity, with dreads covered by a sweatshirt hood, in front of the camera smoking, saying, "Yeah, I shoved a pin through my face. My mom hates it [exhales smoke], but you know, it's rad" (see Figure 3.5).

This opening vignette illustrates some of the ways we worked with the youth at the LOVE site over the course of a year and the lively conversations and ideas

FIGURE 3.5 Kaity in the film *Teenage Kicks*

they brought to the video production workshop. The youth took easily to the medium of filmmaking and quickly figured out how to collect the various multimodal resources they needed to complete a project—pulling images and music from the web, filming each other and the local east side area as a backdrop, using print overlays, editing to convey coherent messages, as well as employing the tools of humor and parody as counter narratives. Here they provide a parody of the common narratives about contemporary youth.

In addition to teaching the skills of video production, we often introduced films by youth in other projects, by our own university students, and from the *Media That Matters* website and commercials to convey various aspects of filmmaking, such as how people and ideas are portrayed, techniques of manipulation, and what is included and elided. The youth drew on their own lives, experiences, and the goals of the program to create films that would speak back to all kinds of violence, including stereotyping, oppression, bullying, and family and sexual violence.

The film *Teenage Kicks* draws on many of these resources. In addition to *Reel Bad Arabs*, we had earlier introduced the film *A Girl Like Me* from *Media That Matters* that addresses the dangers of the stereotyping of Black girls—as being too loud, large, or dark-skinned. But the youth had many of their own experiences with stereotyping and the parodies came easily to them. Max, for instance, talked about the films he liked, particularly those that address Black history, such as *Boyz n the Hood*, though "that was still playing on stereotypes—boys in the ghetto. I like Blacks being empowered or movies like *Crash* that defeat stereotypes." He also talked about watching lots of films on YouTube and being a "technology freak."

The youth understood the irony involved in exploring these stereotypes, which they saw as a type of violence; that is, they had to imitate and parody these "types," which simultaneously reinscribes and possibly reinforces them. However, they used these parodies as counter-narrative tactics because the parody both imitates the target and distances itself through exaggeration or playing the role against type. For instance, Max is a very gentle young man—far removed from what he projected in the film. And Kaity, while looking very tough, "goth" and dangerous, is a thoughtful, socially responsible teen who in fact had a very close relationship with her mother. At the same time, they are playing to an audience in a way that makes the violent aspect apparent—the types of youth that are represented are often read as dangerous, and are stigmatized and worse. In reflecting on the film *Teenage Kicks*, during his interview, Max said he liked the opportunity to work on it and being able to express ideas about "being Black in Vancouver," including assumptions that he is going to steal from a store and that the ways he is sexualized. He also said he hoped that people wouldn't just laugh, but also take the film seriously.

Research on youth video production both in and out of schools now has a fairly long research tradition, including early work by Buckingham and Sefton-Green (1994) and more recent work by Burn and Parker (2003), Goodman (2003), Hull and Greeno (2006), Jocson (2012), Morrell (2007), Kearny (2006) and Rogers, Winters, LaMonde, and Perry (2010). Taken together these studies make visible the ways youth are critically engaged producers of media, who appropriate and transform discursive modes and resources of popular culture at the convergence of old and new media (Jenkins, 2006) for their own purposes. As much of the work of the LOVE youth illustrates, among marginalized youth in particular, media production has been seen as a forum for subverting and rewriting media representations of themselves and others (e.g., Rogers and Schofield, 2005; Rogers et al., 2010; Hull and Greeno, 2006; Morrell, 2007; Jocson, 2012).

The LOVE Program

Leave Out Violence (LOVE) is a community (after-school) anti-violence program in several North American cities, including Vancouver (see http://www. bc.leaveoutviolence.org). The program was started to help youth end violence in their lives and become community leaders of violence prevention. The program was started in 1993 by a woman named "Twinkle" (Sheila) Rudberg after her husband Daniel was killed by a fourteen-year-old gang member on the streets of downtown Montreal. During the trial, Twinkle had learned that the young man was himself a victim of violence, and so she decided to develop a youth violence prevention program, working with a journalist and a photographer. Photojournalism became the core of the program, followed by the creation of a school outreach program. The youth engaged in writing and photojournalism to express the impact of violence in their lives, and helped to prevent further violence through their outreach activities. Participants are self-referred or referred to the program by social service agencies, youth groups, law enforcement agencies, community centers, and schools.

"Our goal is to create safe spaces in which youth can express themselves constructively, through discussion and the creation of media arts, and to develop a cohesive group of Youth Leaders who will use their creations as educational tools throughout our communities" (LOVE, 2013). At the time that we arrived, several of the youth in the group had previously published poetry, photography, and articles in the newspaper, such as Tracei's poem in *ONE L.O.V.E.* (2008) that in many ways represents the kind of resilience and speaking back we often heard at this site:

> I have seen my own power
> Call me what you want
> Break me down to bits
> I can't stop you from acting like a fool
> Cuz' spitting in my face
> Will really make you cool
> And you can't stop me
> From being me
> I am WAY cooler than what you see

You, Dearest one. . .ha ha
You are blind to me
You can't see the strength in my faith
I have seen my own power
What I'm going to do
Is live up to each and every hour.

Leave Out Violence currently has a media arts program, a two-year leadership program, an outreach program, and ongoing violence prevention programming. However, at the time that we met with staff from the program, they had just begun to think about developing a video component in the Vancouver site. During three phases of our yearlong video project, youth at this site created films focused on specific issues related to identity, stereotyping, and anti-violence, and created an outreach film about the LOVE program itself (see Figures 3.6 and 3.7).

FIGURE 3.6 Youth working on films at LOVE center

Credit: Theresa Rogers

FIGURE 3.7 Youth working on films at LOVE center

Credit: Theresa Rogers

Our role in this program was slightly more structured than the work at the street youth site. We began by engaging the group of about fifteen youth, mostly young women in the beginning, in watching and critiquing youth-created films. As described above, we invited the youth to critique various popular film genres (e.g., parodies on YouTube—such as a stop-action music video, and short anti-war or street-life documentaries made by university students and local film-makers). The youth also critiqued films from our previous project site (see Rogers et al., 2010). In their view, several of those films from that previous project were too visually repetitive or, in one case, used too many violent images for a film intended to espouse non-violence (referring to the film *Where Is the Love?* from Rogers et al., 2010). We found this interesting given that this was our own conclusion as researchers—that the youth at the previous site had at times reinscribed violence, racism, and stereotypes in their attempts to counter these very problematic societal discourses. This arts and media work among youth continually prompts us to be open to and to remember the importance of recurring cycles of creation, analysis, and critical re-evaluation in the pedagogical process.

Early in phase one of the project, Anne-Marie, as an accomplished filmmaker, presented some basic elements of filming that drew on their previous work in photojournalism. She began with still images, inviting the youth to utilize the modes of photographic framing and camera zoom found more often in photo-journalism (i.e., documenting) than conceptual or abstract photography. The mode of framing (though operating with the same principles inherent of photo-graphy, i.e., creating positive and negative space) works to capture figure and back-ground in order to frame the human-interest story (the setting), while the camera mode (i.e., zoom) operates to capture perspective.

The youth were then invited to create a narrative based on twenty-four frames (metaphorically based on the number of frames in one second of real film). We suggested they could either build the narrative by selecting stills after shooting a series (not unlike documentary filmmaking) or they could imagine and/or story-board a narrative first and then take a series of still shots (a more familiar form of fictional writing). The next week we brought in video cameras to add film interviews to their narratives as additional footage to deepen the perspectives and/or allow for commentaries. In other words, the video cameras intentionally introduced mixed media forms. We provided ideas for integrating interviews of "characters," "a making of the film" commentary, or adding a director's voice-over (all of which could be modeled on extended features of movies on DVDs). We then taught the youth basic editing skills using iMovie and Apple computers that we supplied. The youth readily picked up the editing skills in a manner typical of learners with extensive exposure to filmic works and familiarity with computers and made use of various visual and sound effects and cutting and montage techniques (e.g., jump cuts, dissolves, fades, etc.).

Violence Remixed

As Lev Manovich (2001) argued in his book, *The Language of New Media*, contemporary media culture brings with it new models of authorship, collaboration, intertexting, and remixing that are evident in these youth video productions. Youth have become flexible users of multimodal cultural forms, such as genres—they borrow, exploit, juxtapose, hybridize, or transform media genres and digital and non-digital spaces for their own critical expression. With the increasing accessibility of open-source cultural materials, such as images, texts, music, etc., hybridizing, digital mashing up, and remixing has become common. An example of this in our project is a film made by Kaity about Billie Holiday. This was one of the first films she made and, while it is simple in its approach, the result is emotionally powerful. Billie Holiday's performance of "Strange Fruit" is well-known and available for viewing on the web (e.g., YouTube). The song is based on a poem by the same name written by Abel Meeropol (pen name Lewis Allen) in 1937. He wrote it after seeing a photograph of the lynching of two African American men in Indiana. The lyrics begin: "Southern trees bear a strange fruit, /Blood on the leaves and blood at the root, /Black bodies swinging in the Southern breeze, /Strange fruit hanging from the poplar trees."

In Kaity's film, Billie Holiday begins singing and the images shift between stock photographs of Billie Holiday at work and the video of her singing, with the images given a "grainy" editing effect. As Kaity's film progresses, Holiday appears to become older and more despairing, both in the photos and the video. At one point the screen goes dark, and in the last scene there is no sound, creating an eerie and foreboding feeling (see Figures 3.8 and 3.9).

FIGURE 3.8 Image from Kaity's Billie Holiday film

FIGURE 3.9 Image from Kaity's Billie Holiday film

While the film is made entirely from Internet images that Kaity then "aged," as she called it, the overall effect of the short film is quite a moving statement about Billie Holiday and her embodiment of the sorrow, as well as the tragedy, of the content. Kaity said she had a "big thing" for Billie Holiday and felt she had a rich and emotional voice that captured despair. She knew that Billie Holiday had been raped and struggled with alcohol—she had seen the film "Lady Sings the Blues." Kaity also said she could identify with her. (The youth in this program often shared their personal stories of violence in the outreach program, though we chose not to recount those stories here.) Kaity also thought that it was amazing and strong for a woman in those days to sing about lynchings.

In describing her technique, Kaity said she wanted to show how Holiday's face moves from happy to almost crying, but how in the end she "gathers herself together and gets off the stage." She wanted to capture the melancholy and show how Holiday was interpreting the words and her reaction to them—"to tell the story of her essence," which she thought people might not otherwise see. For her, the important element was how Billie Holiday interpreted the poem and how she (Kaity) could impose another layer of interpretation to shed light on Billie Holiday, who is a compelling figure to her. Referencing the remixing and mashup of materials, Kaity felt that if you use still pictures, music, lyrics, and filmic elements together it is "better visually . . . if just still pictures are used, it is too much like a slide show." In other words, Kaity was able to use a form of compositional literacy (i.e., an understanding of film composition) that is highly dependent on critical judgment and the careful mounting of images and sound that would best convey her intended message. The use of music with other modalities of film adds another immediate, emotional, or affective layer, expressed and felt through the body, creating lived connections between signs, bodies, and objects (Hull and Nelson, 2005; Leander and Boldt, 2013). In the film she made, Kaity thought you could actually see and feel Holiday interpreting the words she was singing.

In another example of an early film made during the project, two young women, Nichelle and Samara, decided to create a humorous narrative about panhandling for money. In the beginning, it was a designed as a setup to "test" out both the act of panhandling and youth stereotypes. They were not certain but wondered, nevertheless, if anyone passing by would take them at face value. In the end their narrative evolved into a multi-layered account that tells the story of drug use, the means to obtain drugs, and rehabilitation. Their film, *Candyblues*, is a combination of their own video created using the twenty-four-frames approach described earlier, which first depicts the story of a prank panhandling event, followed by an interview of Nichelle, set to a song by Clarence Brown called "Depression Blues." The process began with the two young women exchanging ideas around a personal narrative. Understanding the premise of narrating a story solely through imagery, which draws from graphic storytelling genres (e.g., comics), and being familiar with documentary style photography through their prior photojournalism work, they visualized a sequence of images that would eventually lead to a cautionary tale. They began by taking still shots of the panhandling scenes, which they then parsed down to twenty-four images, and carefully mounted into a narrative, utilizing the concepts of framing (e.g., establishing shots) and perspective (e.g., close-ups, long shots) that we had taught them. For instance, in the establishing shots, they framed the figures and their background as a way to capture a "human-interest" story; they used close-ups—a zoom—of a person panhandling for money (the event), and another of a cardboard sign with a humorous caption (the motive). Later, they inserted parts of the filmed interview intercut throughout the final video, which also served as a form of voice-over to add depth to the story.

In the resulting video, we see an opening title question, which was decided upon in post-production, "How far would you go?" followed by the close-up shots of the sign they created that reads, "Smile ☺ if you masterbate [sic]. Spare change if you love it." To set up the scene, they had taken the sign outside to the street for the "panhandler" to sit with an empty box, testing whether or not they could collect any money panhandling. From the perspective of documentary style filmmaking—journalistic or otherwise—the project was a "set-up" and served to confirm their assumptions, but the resulting story allowed them to play out some of their lived concerns. We will never know whether or not their story might have changed had they not been successful but since they were successful, the narrative gained more ground. The interview sections included Nichelle in the foreground with children on swings in the background filmed in a local park (see Figures 3.10, 3.11, and 3.12).

FIGURE 3.10 Clip 1, a sign from a film by Nichelle and Samara, *Candyblues*

FIGURE 3.11 Clip 2, a box with coins, from a film by Nichelle and Samara, *Candyblues*

FIGURE 3.12 Clip 3, a person walking by, from a film by Nichelle and Samara, *Candyblues*

Later, during an interview, when Samara was reflecting on making the film she said it was "just for fun. We were joking around and were going to go out with a sign and someone suggested the masturbation idea so we got a box." Although we are not able to describe the varying creative processes in filmmaking in detail here, it was clear that they were utilizing a time-honored approach in filmmaking where the serendipitous event often drives the imagery, sound, and narrative. For Nichelle, the film took on a more serious tone in light of the fact that she had been addicted to drugs and had engaged in panhandling. Notably, however, the "seriousness" is couched in a satiric view (view the film at http://blogs.ubc.ca/theresarogersresearch/). The "candy" referred to in the film becomes code for drugs. As Nichelle says in the film while sitting at the playground, "What made me panhandle, eh? Well I needed my fixes for candy . . . so that's why I sat there to get my candy, man." The interviewer then asks, "So did you go to candy rehab?" Nichelle doesn't answer, instead choosing to continue the parody that includes the kids: "Those kids out there, they're like, 'Candy [shouted as a request], I need my candy.' I just can't do that no more, man [rubbing her nose and sniffing]. I'm clean now."

This film represents the playful nature of the kinds of remixing with which the youth were comfortable. To the initial modalities of verbal social exchange, written word, music, and still photography were layered the multiple modalities of filming. These film modalities include post-production titling (i.e., "How far would you go?"), implied movement (e.g., photographic zooming), frame selection (i.e., staging) and additional dialogue recording (i.e., ADR). In addition, the importance of casting, location, and varying modes of address all factor into the character and nature of the overall story.

The choice of including on- and off-screen modes of address follows contemporary forms of journalism (especially in the interview) that create a subjective viewpoint made more "personal" by these modes of address. The contemporary interview genre (versus traditional genre) of journalism reveals the filming process to the viewer, as a way to break the "objective" view produced when awareness of the camera is "suspended." The person now revealed behind the camera becomes part of the process of documenting rather than being an independent "eyewitness" or, in the case of the surveillance camera, independent of a camera operator.

Initially, the images were intended to depict panhandling for money with a comic undertone created by the signage. This approach, as seen in reality television and especially staged for the "candid" comedy camera, allowed them to interact with any passersby invited to put money in their cardboard box. The event provided an inventive twist on a common site in Vancouver—youth on the street with cardboard signs asking for money. By turning the focus on the passerby whose donation would reveal both a sense of humor and what can be considered a private and possibly embarrassing behavior, the shame that mostly accompanies street youth panhandling was diverted. Their intent evolved, however, to play with the word "candy" as a common euphemism for drugs. Several layers of meaning were achieved visually throughout their imagery, from "posing" with a passerby who donated money, to the final series of images depicting the purchase of candy from the money that was panhandled. From the start, the two young women were operating from a sophisticated satirical viewpoint to create their digital story, which progressed ever more complexly as the narrative unfolded.

The result is a rich remixing of modalities and forms or genres. The short video is part confessional, part contemporary journalistic interview, part human-interest story or biography, part historical documentary (blues song), part satire, and includes overlapping cautionary tales.

We include historical documentary, which was enabled through the choice of a blues song with reference to "hard times" during the Great Depression, as it was juxtaposed with images of contemporary "hard times" (i.e., panhandling on the street). The youth were fully aware of the ways socio-economic class is unevenly and unfairly related to the effects of economic downturns and the ever-present marginalization and personal struggles of those with fewer resources in Vancouver, a contemporary global city.

Countering Violence: Embodied Youth in the City

As illustrated above, the LOVE youth, like the street youth, drew on their embodied subjectivities along with the tools of irony, parody, and satire to both position themselves in the world and to critique larger discourses and practices. The films described on panhandling and drug use, Billie Holiday, and stereotyping all have clear ironic, satiric, and critical elements related to poverty and violence and contain particular embodied race, class, and gender representations, though these are not always foregrounded. The films described below by two young women, Tracei and Kaity, further address issues of embodied youth and countering violence.

Tracei, a young woman in the project who had also experienced violence in her life, and often alluded to it during our sessions together, provides a close look at a representation of critical embodied girlhood (Kendrick et al., 2010). Early in the project, Tracei made an "identity" video titled *I are Tracei, hear me roar!* Through a series of still images, Tracei chronicles her transformation from a traditionally wholesome looking young girl to a young woman with multicolored hair and facial piercings that, she said, conveyed her as "all crazy and older." In this mashup video, she uses a song from a third-wave ska band (The Madd Caddies) titled "Mary Melody" to reinforce her message. The coda is: "I showed you Tracei, now take it!" Tracei commented later that her idea was to go back in time and ask, "What happened to my innocence?" Indeed, this film clearly provides a counter narrative to the blond girl as innocent, silent, and passive and reinscribes her body and her discourse with a message of strength, resilience, and resistance (see Figures 3.13, 3.14, and 3.15).

FIGURE 3.13 Clip 1, title from Tracei's *I are Tracei* film

FIGURE 3.14 Clip 2, early photo from Tracei's *I are Tracei* film

FIGURE 3.15 Clip 3, recent photo from Tracei's *I are Tracei* film

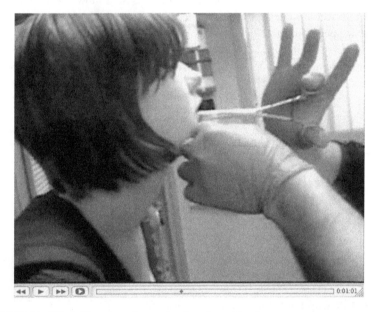

FIGURE 3.16 Clip 1, Tracei getting a piercing, from *Traceiisawesome*

Shortly after finishing this first video, Tracei sent us another video that she made from home titled *Traceisawesome*. The accompanying message is, "I wanted to share something with you." This second video, which is analyzed here, can be seen as a "publicly private film" (Lange, 2007) that provided a way to recognize an even more complex set of identity positions that Tracei took up in her life. Tracei referred to her passion for taking pictures and filmmaking, which she often did on her own and with friends. She wanted us to see another, more complex rendering of her identity—one that is usually available only to her peers.

This film has three distinct scenes (see representative still images in Figures 3.16–3.18). The first scene includes two extended and close-up filmed shots of

0:01:47

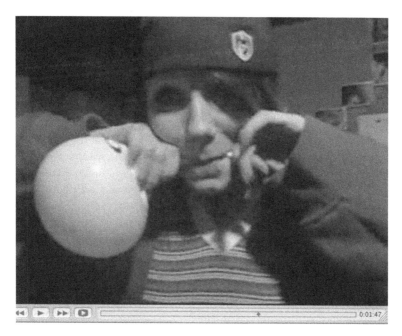

FIGURE 3.17 Clip 2, Tracei with balloon, from *Traceiisawesome*

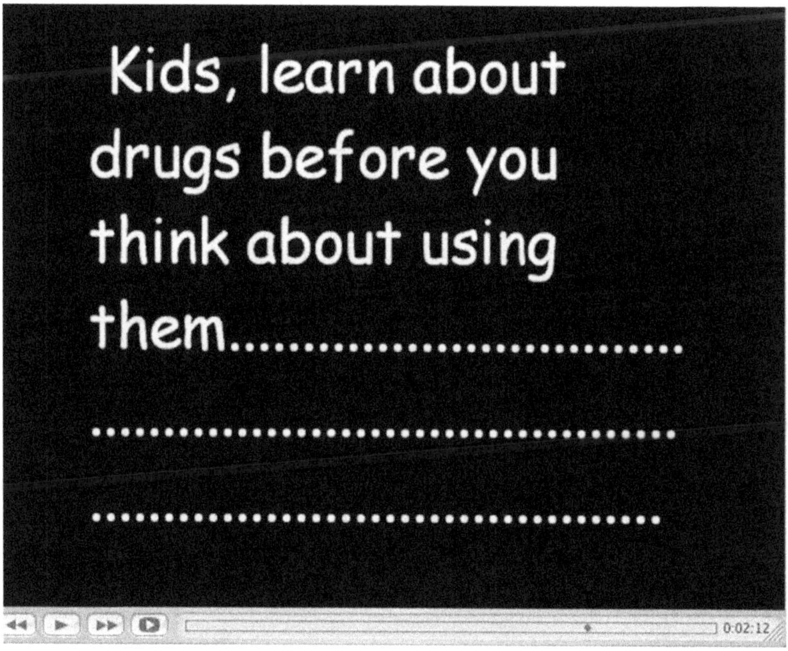

Kids, learn about drugs before you think about using them.......................................
0:02:12

FIGURE 3.18 Clip 3, text from *Traceiisawesome*

Tracei's bottom lip being pierced (Figure 3.16). The second scene is a filmed shot of Tracei singing, laughing, and talking with a helium voice [to friends behind the camera who can be heard giggling], saying "I don't know what to say. Hey you guys are putting pressure on me. What am I going to do? I'm gonna sit here an' cry making emo songs, gonna die, this is gonna make me fall over. It's gonna hurt. I'm done" (Figure 3.17). The third section of the film, which also serves as a kind of coda, is a mixture of print messages and photos of herself with her friends, and one still shot of her dressed in drag. This section begins with the text "the end" and continues with "This video was made to prevent the use of chemically made drugs" and "Kids, learn about drugs before you think about using them . . . These kids didn't have a clue what they were doing." After several more photo sequences it ends with "save yourselves! Before it's too late" (Figure 3.18).

In the film Tracei draws on several cultural forms and layers various modes of expression to engage in fluid subject positionings within what she sees as available storylines (Davies and Harre, 1990). In many respects Tracei is using these resources to enact a form of temporary agency by moving between one set of socially and culturally formed subjectivities to another. As Holland et al. (1998) argue, individuals enact these forms of agency through hope, desperation, or play. The result is a sense of resistant playfulness with identity, genres, and modalities that results in a counter narrative to given representations of girlhood.

This film, as a whole, is a fascinating representation of resistant feminine subjectivity. The literal embodiment of expression and resistance to normalized feminine behavior through piercings, hair color, and cross-dressing is evident. Drawing on popular culture and using new media provides her tools to parody gender identity and to engage in social commentary and critique (Buckingham and Sefton-Green, 1994): the choice of music playfully draws on her interest in film and TV genres of horror. She uses the "Freaker's Ball" song by the '70s rock band Dr. Hook and the Medicine Show—itself a parody of the '60s countercultural love-ins. The film becomes even more complex when she satirizes "emo" behavior and appropriates discursive resources of popular media to parody the use of public service announcements (PSA) with anti-drug messages. When asked about her use of print in her films she said, "words help get the point across. Some people can be totally oblivious but once they read it, they say 'oh, I get it.'" She also commented that she liked to get together with friends to make PSAs and "stuff like that and get it out there."

Within this kind of identity and cultural work, adolescent bodies often represent lived realities (Grosz, 1994); that is, the body is further inscribed with information about youth subjectivity and positioning in their work and in their lives. Viewed this way, media can be a particularly productive space for appropriating, refiguring, and imagining these embodiments (Ellsworth, 2005; Grosz and Eisenman, 2001). In fact, the fluid spaces between the body and media provide the body "new forms of corporeality" (Ellsworth, 2005, pp. 125–126) and forms of address and possibilities of living differently.

Tracei's embodied visual production inscribes and repositions her in parodic and resistant poses to larger cultural narratives of gender; the images provide a private/public space for writing dissent on her body through piercing, the balloon performance, and presenting herself in drag. This dissent, in its representation of the complexity of girlhood and appropriation of stereotypes, cultural tropes, and multimodal resources, can be seen as a form of private production as well as a more public counter discourse of contemporary girlhood. Like other youth in this project, Tracei skillfully poaches and plays with a range of discursive and cultural resources to engage in or talk back to dominant cultural narratives about her life and her social worlds.

In another example of a critical counter narrative, Kaity imagined a film she would like to make during our interview with her in which bodies in the city are temporary encoded to fix them in the face of a changing landscape. She said:

> I have a couple of ideas for five-minute films. I want to do one to the song by Air (the band) called "People in the City," and just film all these people in Vancouver to just kind of like show the variety and, before the Olympics hit, like people doing weird things like showing people asleep on the bus, just like little things that people always forget about. Like I want to do a shot of people busking on the streets. I want to do a shot of some businessmen. Because they are big part of Vancouver. Um, kids smoking pot at the art gallery, people just waiting for the bus, people on their cellphones, people drinking Starbucks, people—like kids, crazy crackheads, like kids smoking crack on Granville. Kids hanging out in the Kitslano area. Just like film different areas and put it to the song . . . I can speed it up and slow it down, like I want to do some skytrain shots during rush hour and it would be cool having these people coming in and out and slowing down and speeding it up . . . It's gonna change. They're tearing down theatres, like the one across the street [a local arts and second-run movie theatre] and I'm like why? And they said they need more condos and I'm like it's Vancouver, we have enough condos, and like they're trying to ban buskers which is a tourist attraction, bad idea. And like they're taking down low-income housing, a lot of it, which kinda sucks, like some people can't afford it and it's like the rich get richer and the poor get poorer, and if your too poor to live here then see ya later, pretty much. Renovating everything. Everything's going to be really extensive so it's either gonna be people thriving or a lot of people are gonna have to leave. The city's losing a lot of character and I want to capture it before it changes and shatters into pieces. They are taking down a lot of small independent stuff and everything is like shiny and new and flashy and glass and trendy. That's what they are planning for it [Vancouver] to be.

What Kaity is describing for her film is the gentrification of her global city in a particular moment in time—a period before the hosting of the Olympics. Kaity refers to what *Hollow City* authors, Solnit and Schwartzenberg (2000) portray as the "homogenization of the city . . . the decay of public life and the erasure of sites of memory" in San Francisco, and the ways "wealth is clearcutting the cultural richness of American urban life, erasing space for idealism, dissent, memory and vulnerable populations" (from the front cover). In *Hollow City*, the authors, an historian and photographer document what they consider a crisis in American cities and argue that visual artists are a barometer of the loss of artistic, political, spiritual, and social activity.

Indeed, the youth were exquisitely sensitive to their community surroundings and changes. Their work, as well as a sense of self and imagined social futures and possibilities—across all three sites—was meditated by the community (e.g., James, 2012). And if youth are social subjects who are created and create themselves in and through the social space of the city (Ruddick, 1998), the control of public space and resources affect those imagined futures. In this context, youth arts, literacy, and media practices become tactics (de Certeau, 1984) that recuperate the symbolic meaning of spaces as a kind of resistance. Kaity's film description becomes a form of narrative testimonial of a contemporary urban imaginary (Dillabough and Kennelly, 2010), focusing on the variety of embodied and spacialized youth (busking in the streets, smoking pot at the art gallery lawn, hanging out in Kits, sleeping on buses) who will likely be displaced. Indeed, much of what Kaity described continued in the lead-up to and after the 2010 Olympics in Vancouver. The economic disparity grows wider, housing is increasingly unaffordable for all but richest inhabitants, and gentrification pushes at the boundaries of communities, erasing local cultural life and creating more spaces that are "shiny and new and flashy and glass and trendy."

Taking Anti-Violence Work to the Schools, Community, and Nation

The purpose of the photojournalism and media aspects of the LOVE programming is for youth "to learn to become reporters on youth culture and violence and to voice their own experiences . . . the program creates change at the individual and societal level" (from the LOVE marketing materials). Additional stated goals are to create an environment for youth to feel safe to open up and talk, to unite victims, perpetrators, and witnesses to explore the realities of youth violence, to help youth understand the social context of their behavior, to make a difference, and to break down barriers among youth, such as race, class, sexual orientation, gender, age, etc. In addition to publishing their work in the *ONE L.O.V.E.* newspaper, they publish books (*LOVE Works!*; *The Courage to Changes: A Teen Survival Guide*) and other materials.

The photojournalism and media training programming is followed by leadership training where the youth build skills for public speaking and are further educated on issues such as gangs, substance abuse, dating violence, self-esteem, equity issues, and bullying. Once completed, the youth are then invited to lead school and community outreach presentations to students and adults in schools and community educational sites, and to decision-makers in business and government.

Toward the end of our project three of the youth participated in an outreach workshop for university students in the counseling education program. The panel began with each youth sharing their story and then responding to questions from the instructor and the students. This event was filmed so the youth could include it in the final phase of our project with them, which was the creation of an outreach video. One of the youth, Lyla, was an experienced outreach leader and was also instrumental in helping to plan and create the final video.

The youth wanted to create an outreach video that would be a compilation representing the kind of work that they engaged in and produced in the program. At the first meeting of those interested in this culminating project, we began by showing some clips from LOVE interview videos taken in the past. Anne-Marie pointed out aspects that were done well, such as framing, but also pointed out when there was too much headroom above the face to capture a sense of the intimate. The larger the face on screen (i.e., the tighter the close-up), the more emotionally compelling it is for an audience—a factor that would draw an audience into the text. Anne-Marie then shared possible techniques they might use for their film, such as zooming and dynamic shots produced by utilizing a handheld technique versus using a tripod to steady the shot.

A discussion then ensued about what genre the film might be (or ought to be), which would ultimately drive the kind of footage that would be needed—"a documentary mix?" (Anne-Marie); "A point-of-view piece?" (Jen); "like a commercial—like the ones by MADD?" (Tracei) "Or joining the army . . . or something like Billy Talent's 'Red Flag'?" (Kaity). They eventually decided to include mixed footage: an interview with Lyla, a youth member of the original Vancouver program, alongside archived photographs of the original group of youth, followed by photos and clips of recent outreach events along with words overlaid, such as "Love, respect, energy" (suggested by Sara, the current program leader), and any other archived or current video that represented the group. Anne-Marie suggested that they take all the ideas and storyboard the structure of the film.

They decided to call the film *A Taste of LOVE* and to include establishing images, film clips from their outreach work in the schools and the university, individual stories and interviews, and photographs with overlays and short films representing who they are through words and images. Interestingly, they talked about whether or not the film would turn out to be a "corporate film"—by which they meant a promotional video that adults would view and relate to that could also function as a fundraising tool. Or, in contrast, they wondered whether the video would turn out to be more "youth-oriented"—that would be less formal and more DIY, more artsy and emotional, and could be used in their outreach program. It was clear from the discussion that they believed the film would turn out to be one or the other and could not accomplish both genres at the same time. The completed film brings out the emotional qualities they mentioned and is more descriptive of the latter, though it was eventually shown as part of a public fundraising event, which took place at a café that included spoken-word performances, music, and sales of photography as well as the public screening of the film. While not quite "corporate-like," the film possessed a quality that raised a sense of responsibility toward the support of youth-run programs capable of such vibrant expression.

Various youth volunteered to film, edit, supply sound, or assist others. Across the weeks of planning this final video, we supported the youth by brainstorming ideas about, for instance, words they might use to describe violence (e.g., kinds of abuses, isms, and self-harm) and words that describe their hopes and their program (e.g., truthful, happy, passionate, unbreakable). We also filmed Lyla's interview, helped them download images and clips from outreach events, and helped them refine the storyboard, select music, and edit the film. Though Anne-Marie handled some of the final edits in order to help them achieve their desired outcome, their rough edits and ideas, along with their general direction, were honored. This collaboration demonstrated a common post-production relationship between the visionary director(s) and the post-production technique of the editor(s). It was clear to the youth that the final cut would ultimately determine the genre, which was told in varying stages across time.

The final eight-minute film begins with a rapid succession of eleven still images of the LOVE youth and their program leaders speaking at outreach events. Each still is titled with animated words that bounce and spin across the screen: *Interactive, Eye-opening, Inspirational, Informative, Thoughtful, Engaging, Provocative, Peer to Peer, Real, Supportive,* and *Empowering* (see Figures 3.19–3.21). These images and words

FIGURE 3.19 Clip 1, "Interactive," from *A Taste of LOVE*

FIGURE 3.20 Clip 2, "Thoughtful," from *A Taste of LOVE*

FIGURE 3.21 Clip 3 "Empowering," from *A Taste of LOVE*

are set to the song, "Something's Got a Hold on Me (It Must Be Love)," by Etta James. The film then moves to a section titled "Early stages of LOVE" and shows old clips of some of the original youth in the project, followed by an interview clip of Lyla (with the song fading out and ending as Lyla's clip begins).

The next scene is Max telling his life story at an outreach event in a secondary school. In the clip you can hear him talk about moving from Montreal, and though he did not speak English he was sent to an English school. He talks about how other kids teased him and he had trouble learning at first.

This is followed by current youth in the project each saying one word related to violence in their lives with their faces hidden behind hoods or hats: violence, racism, depression, bullying, self-harm, alcohol, sexism, set to the song "Needle in the Hay," by Elliot Smith. These images are interspersed with photos from the wall of the program center (see Figures 3.1 and 3.2 at the beginning of chapter). They each then pull their hats or hoods away to show their faces; the young man in the last shot says "We are youth" and cuts to a kiss between two youth and the whiteboard with the words "Leave Out Violence" being written, and lists of participants (see Figures 3.22–3.24).

The next clip is Lyla talking about how almost everyone is affected by violence in some way as victim, perpetrator, or witness. "We learn how to tell our story in a safe and supportive program . . . it becomes like a family." The whiteboard image reappears with "WE Are . . . ," followed by changing descriptors such as: *truthful, gay (happy), united as one, we are the future, you are not alone.* The final clip in this section is of two youth hugging. The "WE ARE . . ." whiteboard image returns

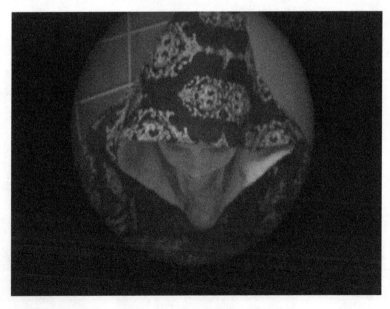

FIGURE 3.22 Clip 4, from the film *A Taste of LOVE*

FIGURE 3.23 Clip 5, from the film *A Taste of LOVE*

FIGURE 3.24 Clip 6, from the film *A Taste of LOVE*

with the descriptors: *youth of the nation, unbreakable, passionate, believers, amazingly awesome, family, L O V E.*

The film ends with a lengthy listing of film credits to all "who helped to make the film" set to the song "All You Need Is Love," by the Beatles, and a final clip of Lyla joking about the name of the program "It's a common joke—I'm in love, are you?—how long have you been in love?" The song "Something's Got a Hold on Me" returns with the words: "Thanks goes out to all the L.O.V.E youth then and now who passionately speak today about Leave Out Violence" (see http://blogs.ubc.ca/theresarogersresearch/).

The film was warmly received at the fundraising event with lots of cheering by the youth. There was a palpable sense of pride toward the making of the film by the group of filmmakers who gathered in a tight-knit group, but also a tremendous joy that was shown by former members of the LOVE community and accompanying adults. Several former members honored the newest members by hugging and showing great affection, as well as sharing a few anecdotes publicly. The event included the sale of photographs by the youth, calendars, newspapers, and other LOVE artifacts. In the end, the film was clearly more of a "youth-oriented" DIY film, rather than the more polished films that are featured on the Leave Out Violence website, such as those made in collaboration with film schools, many of which are testimonies of success. But the event generated strong interest in the program, which satisfied Lyla and her group—each of whom expressed that their collaboration and effort had been a great success.

Activism and civic engagement are at the core of the LOVE programming. The youth were comfortable with reaching out to other youth and adults. They often shared their written stories at outreach evenings; as Kaity commented, "Reading it out lives it, and it's empowering." They were eager to find a means to get their films out in the public as well. As Max said, he wanted his work to be funny but also taken seriously. In her interview, Kaity provided an extended commentary on the need for youth activism in Vancouver. She felt that youth needed to "take the bull by the horns" and take responsibility for things rather than "just bitching about bad decisions."

> We need to take our own destiny into our own hands . . . I have a voice just like any big office chairman. . . . Like that stupid Olympic countdown clock downtown. It's hideous and they're paying a security guard to watch it. You know why? Because all the civilians want to take it down. People did a peaceful protest and they cuffed them. They say it's gonna be good for the city. For who? . . . And, like. I talked to the school board, the head of the school board, about their drug policies. And I'm like, you need to treat us like equals. We treat you like equals and you treat us as less than. Like when you get suspended for smoking pot at schools, what happens? We are trying to change it so it is more like counseling rather than sending them home and letting them sit in their rooms and smoke more pot. Even though I'm pro-marijuana—I don't smoke it anymore—but they are doing stupid stuff. They need to educate people more about the ecstasy and meth that's out there. You can get hooked on meth. Give them the downlow before they try it. Youth could do a better job educating younger people. . . . It's in the community. We live in Vansterdam. People celebrate 4/20 at the art gallery and half the city shows up. If they have the right information they would know not to take it further.

As with the street youth we worked with, the LOVE youth were engaged in public life and used the hybrid discursive resources of writing, art, and film to speak out and confront oppression and violence in homes and communities. They often employed the tools of irony, parody, and satire to strengthen their messages as in the stereotypes film and the panhandling film. The fact that those particular literary modes have often been utilized by the voiceless and oppressed was not lost on them for, like Kaity, many were tuned into both the historical and contemporary forms of these genres. They rewrote perceived representations of youth, and pushed against the devaluing of their own voice and perspectives. They often used sophisticated historical imagery and music to deepen their analyses and representations of the visible current economic inequities.

The LOVE youth reached out to larger and smaller publics through their lived and embodied stories and performances, creating new forms of aesthetic and engaged citizenship (Boler, 2008; Hickey-Moody, 2013; Warner, 2002), through a complex discursive form of civic participation that is "more than local but less than global" (Pinny, 2001, cited in Dillabough and Kennelly, 2010, p 4). Most, but not all, of the youth in this project were living with less precariousness than the street youth; yet they also sought to be seen and heard, to be recognized and legitimized; they displayed their desire for recuperation of public life in a post-industrial global city that is the site of increasing inequality and fragmentation of communities and families, thus increasing the potential of violence in its many forms. In the closing chapter, we further theorize the work of youth at this site in relation to other sites and the implications for understanding the relationship arts, media, and critical literacy practices of youth, public pedagogy, and the intersections of local and global participation in democratic citizenship.

Note

1 LOVE—Leave Out Violence—has as its mission to "reduce violence in the lives of youth in our communities by building a team of youth who communicate a message of nonviolence." LOVE is located in Vancouver, New York, Halifax, Toronto, and Montreal. Youth participate in a variety of media projects and provide outreach to schools.

References

Boler, M. (2008). *Digital media and democracy*. Toronto: University of Toronto Press.

Buckingham, D., & Sefton-Green, J. (1994). *Cultural studies goes to school*. Bristol: Taylor & Francis.

Burn, A., & Parker, D. (2003). *Analysing media texts*. London: Continuum.

Davies, B., & Harre, R. (1990). Positioning: The discursive production of selves. *Journal for the Theory of Social Behaviour, 20*(1), 43–63.

de Certeau, M. (1984). *The practice of everyday life*. Berkeley: University of California Press.

Dillabough, J., & Kennelly, J. (2010). *Lost youth in the global city: Class, culture and the urban imaginary*. New York: Routledge.

Ellsworth, E. (2005). *Places of learning: Media architecture pedagogy.* New York: RoutledgeFalmer.

Goodman, S. (2003). *Teaching youth media: A critical guide to literacy, video production and social change.* New York: Teachers College Press.

Grosz, E. (1994). *Volatile bodies: Toward a corporeal feminism.* Bloomington: Indiana University Press.

Grosz, E., & Eisenman, P. (2001). *Architecture from the outside: Essays on virtual and real space.* Cambridge, MA: MIT Press.

Hickey-Moody, A. (2013). *Youth, arts and education: Reassembling subjectivity through affect.* New York: Routledge.

Holland, D., Lachicotte, W., Skinner, D., & Cain, C. (1998). *Identity and agency in cultural worlds.* Cambridge, MA: Harvard University Press.

Hull, G., & Greeno, J. G. (2006). Identity and agency in non-school and school worlds. In Z. Bekerman, N. Burbules, & D. Silberman-Keller (Eds.), *Learning in places: The informal education reader* (pp. 77–97). New York: Peter Lang.

Hull, G., & Nelson, M. E. (2005). Locating the semiotic power of multimodality. *Written Communication, 22,* 224–261.

James, C. (2012). *Life at the intersection: Community, class and schooling.* Halifax & Winnipeg: Fernwood Publishing.

Jenkins, H. (2006). *Convergence culture: Where old and new media collide.* New York: NYU Press.

Jocson, K. (2012). Youth media as narrative assemblage: Examining new literacies at an urban high school. *Pedagogies: An International Journal, 7*(4), 298–316.

Kearney, M. (2006). *Girls make media.* New York: Routledge.

Kendrick, M., Rogers, T., Toohey, K., Marshall, E., Mutonyi, H., Hauge, C., Siegel, M., Rowsell, J. (2010). Experiments in visual analysis: (Re)positionings of children and youth in relation to larger sociocultural issues. In *59th National Reading Conference Yearbook* (pp. 395–408). Oak Creek, WI: National Reading Conference.

Lange, P. (2007). Publicly private and privately public: Social networking on YouTube. *Journal of Computer-Mediated Communication, 13*(1), 361–380.

Leander, K., & Boldt, G. (2013). Rereading "a pedagogy of multiliteracies": Bodies, texts and emergence. *Journal of Literacy Research, 45*(1), 22–46.

LOVE. (2013). About LOVE. Retrieved April 10, 2014, from http://leaveoutviolence.org/

Manovich, L. (2001). *The language of new media.* Cambridge, MA: MIT Press.

Morrell, M. (2007). *Critical literacy and urban youth.* New York: Routledge.

Pinny, C. (2001). In Dwyer, R. and Pinny, C. (Eds.) *Pleasure and the nation: The history, politics and consumption of public culture in India* (pp. 1–34). London: RoutledgeFalmer.

Rogers, T., & Schofield, A. (2005). Things thicker than words: Portraits of youth multiple literacies in an alternative secondary program. In J. Anderson, M. Kendrick, T. Rogers, & S. Smythe (Eds.), *Portraits of literacy across families, communities and schools* (pp. 205–220). Mahwah, NJ: Lawrence Erlbaum Associates.

Rogers, T., Winters, K. L., LaMonde, A. M., & Perry, M. (2010). From image to ideology: Analysing shifting identity positions of marginalized youth across the cultural sites of video production. *Pedagogies: An International Journal, 5*(4), 298–312.

Ruddick, S. (1998). Modernism and resistance: How "homeless" youth sub-cultures make a difference. In T. Skelton & G. Valentine (Eds.), *Cool places: Geographies of youth cultures* (pp. 343–360). London: Routledge.

Solnit, R., & Schwartzenberg, S. (2000). *Hollow city: The siege of San Francisco and the crisis of American urbanism.* New York: Verso.

Warner, M. (2002). Publics and counterpublics. *Public Culture, 14*(1), 49–90.

4

PERFORMING ADOLESCENCE

Staging Bodies in Motion

> In each character in each piece, there's a bit of everyone.
>
> *Diane in the post-performance talk-back discussion*

The drama class at Lismore Secondary School (pseudonym) was made up of fifteen grade 9 students (eleven girls and four boys) in addition to two grade 12 students who were there to develop directing and stage management skills. The school was located in a middle class area a few miles north of the city, and the students were a White, Indo-Canadian, and from other less visible ethnic groups. The classroom doubled as the school studio theatre space: A "black box" auditorium/rehearsal room with the flexibility of open floors, spotlights, sound equipment, and tiered seating. During a typical class backpacks were strewn everywhere and the teacher's desk sat in the corner of the space, equipped with a computer and the various accoutrements of a teacher's headquarters. The contrast with the lines of desks and bright lights of every other classroom in the school created an element of possibility in this space. The fundamental opening of floor space suggests that bodies are to be seen and engaged with here. The dark walls, floors, and drapes for exits and entrances invite possibilities of play, pretend, concealment, and in short, *layers* of reality.

On many days the class began in the open space between the drawn-back curtains and the backdrop with warm-up exercises, reflections on the work they had done so far, and discussions about what was working and what wasn't for the students and teachers. As the date approached for the scheduled performance, the students were struggling with the idea of devising a play and this process of performance creation, questioning an approach that they were unfamiliar with. They were more accustomed to traditional performances, such as Shakespeare's *Twelfth Night*, or popular plays, such as *Oklahoma*, that took place each spring at their school. On this particular day, the students were asked to group themselves, in character, with other characters who might possibly share the same timeframe (medieval times, contemporary time), or context (young aspiring artists in contemporary city, princesses and Scottish lords). The students were going to begin creating scenes that might be included in the final public performance scheduled to take place a few months later. The performance would be entirely devised by students with the support of Mia and their teacher, and occasional visiting co-researchers and educators specializing in movement and dance, lighting, and staging.

In the week leading up to this day, Mia had asked the students, through a number of preliminary exercises and discussions, to identify a series of ideas, concepts, and subjects that they deemed important to them, as individuals and as a group. The first building block of the character development work was a self-selected word or phrase chosen from this list. Mia then asked the students to imagine someone (a character) who might share a strong interest in this idea or theme.

The students engaged in the process of creating characters through their bodies, physically exploring an alternative way of moving and interacting in the space. They further developed the characters through narrative—i.e. writing textual biographies. Mia then asked them to put their characters in relation to others in creation through conversation, interview, and finally scene creation.

In some cases the characters revealed aspirations of their student-creators, in others the character development process was an exploration down a path that was possible in their own lives, in sight, but forbidden or foreboding. Some examples of this relationship between student and character came up with regard to appearance. As Lisa said: "She's like me, but without braces"; Sam commented that: "He's like me, but he's six foot tall." Often age was a distinguishing factor: A fourteen-year-old student becomes twenty-seven.

Mia worked with the students as they more fully developed their characters in relation to others through conversation, interview, and finally scene creation. During this informal, loosely structured exercise, five young women came together with the rough assumption that they would have things in common due to their characters' ages, gender, and interests. In developing a scene that would put these characters in a common space, the girls decided to create a scene in a medical clinic. The initial devising and rehearsal of this scene took place in the foyer outside the theatre in the early spring. The following description is how the scene unfolded during the final performance in June.

The scene opens with Amy, in the role of a clinic receptionist (Emma), entering the performance space to set up a desk, with a laptop, trash can, desk lamp, and coat hanger—traditional symbols of a public, administrative space. She straightens her skirt and sits down. Lexa (played by April) is already seated, waiting, in a plastic chair. The projected backdrop is a large full-bloom flower on the screen, contemporary "indie" music playing during this transition. Following Lexa's entrance, Roxy (character), played by Kim, enters arguing with someone on her cell phone. She stops at the receptionist's table to provide her name and reason for being in the clinic, which she states is blood testing. She takes a seat and finishes her phone call, which is later revealed to have been an argument with her boyfriend. The third performer in the scene portrays Rheanna, a young mother. The fourth to enter is Helen (student) who plays the character Nicky, sixteen years old. Nicky discreetly reports that she is there for a pregnancy test; the receptionist says loudly, "For what?" and so Nicky is forced to repeat, in a way now audible for everyone, that she is there for a pregnancy test.

EMMA: Sorry, what was that?
NICKY: Pregnancy test.
EMMA: Ok, take a seat.
ROXY: (to Nicky) Wow don't you think you're a little young there?
NICKY: Not really
RHEANNA: (to Roxy) Do you have a problem with that?
ROXY: Well she looks about sixteen, I'm just sayin'.

This opening vignette provides a snapshot of how we worked with the students to create a devised theatre performance at Lismore over the course of the year. The sequence of the clinic scene illustrates the way the students took on roles of young women slightly older than themselves and, in their own reproducing of normative societal discourses, they reveal a critical awareness of the ways that the female body is monitored and regulated and a subject of public scrutiny. In this context, Roxy's comments can be seen to be voicing normalizing cultural discourses in response to teenage pregnancy. This tension was criticized by fellow students early on in the development of the work, but remained an important aspect of the scene for the performers, as they wanted to maintain contradictions within the characters. As a result, the discourses represented in this clinic space complicate notions of "urban" girlhood and womanhood—what is normal, what is transgressive (see Figure 4.1).

FIGURE 4.1 Clinic scene

The "clinic-hospital" is one site in which women's bodies are constructed by the ideas around them (e.g., medical narratives) and where we might reconstruct those narratives as "maps of power and identity" (Haraway, 1983, para. 45). In her final interview, Kim (who played Roxy) talks about why the location for the imagined scene made sense to her as one in which they could express issues that might not otherwise be expressible:

> Well, when we first put it together, we thought of, like, how can we get a whole bunch of people kind of admitting their problems, right? And then I was thinking, well, what is a place that you—that would show your problems without even saying anything. And I thought, well, a doctor's office or something, right. And I find that when you're surrounded by strangers sometimes you can just say things because—or do things 'cause you probably won't see them again or something. And what does it matter, they don't really know you and they won't really affect you. So, I don't know, that kind of meant something to our characters 'cause we would act differently around strangers than people that we respected more so or were intimidated by so . . .

The students were aware of the ways the monitoring and negotiation of discourses occurs both inside and outside of the performed scene. Inside the scene, Lexa (character) proceeded from the above quoted interaction, by stating, "Thank God I had an abortion." This statement of positioning and experience provides an alternative response to teenage pregnancy, one that is left unquestioned by the other young female characters in the scene, but that emerges as defiant and taboo in the broader classroom/school space. A school teacher present during a rehearsal of this scene brought attention to the implicit expectations and perimeters of acceptability in the representations presented by these youth by cautioning them, particularly in relation to the "flippant remark about abortion," that they may get a strong response from their audience and to keep that in mind as they develop the script.

In the same conversation, the students were asked where their ideas for characters and scenarios came from. Kim replied, "real life," but immediately adjusted her answer with "no, just kidding." This response resulted in much laughter and cheering from the class. The class interactions outside of, and about, the performed scene and characters revealed the tensions and limits around what can be voiced in a school context.

What took place in the scene and the surrounding class discussions and interviews is a careful negotiation along the borders of normative and transgressive discourses. A balance of sorts was struck between the students' desires to play in transgressive subjectivities and discourses, and their need to maintain the "container" of normative (and in their case, more familiar) behaviors and positions. Simultaneous to the testing and negotiating of discursive boundaries taking place, the constructions and experiences of the feminine urban subject were being complicated as they were put in relation to the students' own subjectivities and positions. In other words, in this case the perceived urban feminine subjectivities were removed from the stable position of "other" and incorporated into a more fluid, contingent position of relation.

Ultimately the girls in this clinic scene—April, Amy, Kim, Dana, and Helen—engaged in remapping and reinscribing their lived and embodied subjectivities through exploring and representing aspects of themselves in relation to known and imagined realities removed from, but proximal, to their own. Inherent in this embodied performance is a critique of normative discourses and structures that limit expressions of youth and gender. In her final interview, April (who plays Lexa) said, "I thought we wouldn't really be allowed to put those kind of things in, like, when we first did our clinic scene, we put a few interesting things in there. But we were surprised that we were allowed to do that, I guess, 'cause it is in school . . ."

Lismore Secondary School Drama Program

At Lismore Secondary School our project focused specifically on devised theatre as a site of inquiry and critique. The devising project was carried out in the ninth-grade drama program over the course of one school year, between September and June. As co-researchers in this site, our roles were changeable and dependent on the circumstances and needs of the site on a day-to-day basis. Overall, we moved along a continuum with participant/observer at one end (Theresa) and facilitator and performance director at the other (Mia). Over the course of the study Mia co-facilitated at least two out of three drama classes per week and supervised two evening theatre outings. We acknowledge this dynamic presence in the project and position ourselves in the same space of interrelational creation that the youth engaged in. In this way, we, as researchers, were implicated along with the youth, and the social, political, cultural, and interpersonal contexts of this project site, perhaps even more than in the context of the other two sites.

As with the other two sites, we used jottings about the performance creation work and discussions that took place that we later turned into field notes. We also videotaped and audiotaped selected class sessions and the final performance, conducted individual interviews, and collected student generated artifacts, such as ongoing written reflections and photographs.

Our relationship with the drama program at Lismore began with an affiliation, and affinity, with the teacher of the program through her graduate study in education. She expressed an interest in learning more about devised theatre, the affordances of the approach, and the possibilities of engaging with it in her current program. The opportunity therefore arose for an exchange of sorts; we as a research team were able to take our theatre and facilitation skills into a classroom in exchange for working with the students for a year to document and analyze the process and products of their engagement with the form.

This relationship between research and the field (schools) is a very common one in educational research; also common is the tensions and negotiations that go along with it. In addition to the expected tensions of guests (from the university) into a classroom who contribute to, and alter, the shape, outcomes, and dynamics of a class, this site involved tensions specifically related to the nature of the work carried out. The process of creation in devised theatre, as we undertook it, depends on emergent and unprescribed processes and outcomes. This fundamental aspect of the work creates challenges to the realities of classroom planning, evaluation, and sometimes even to classroom management in secondary drama education. In addition, we took up the raw materials, or the subtexts, for devising as the subjectivities, the interrelationalities, and the bodies of the participants in the room. On this basis, the extent of what can or could be explored or represented is boundless. The absence of restriction presents obvious challenges to formal education, and involves the risk of uncensored, unsanctioned performances (broadly defined).

We worked with the students on devised theatre creation, including three phases consisting of development of theatre tools, spectatorship, and performance creation. Devised theatre is a sprawling category, with practices and interpretations varying from continent to continent as well as from theatre company to theatre company. It is a form of theatre that has become, over the past two decades, established and widely practiced. "Postmodern" and "postdramatic" have both been used to describe devised theatre and its various performative relatives, and terms and definitions continue to swirl in the theory and critique of the practice. As a general rule, devised theatre is the creation of original work or the re-imagining of traditional texts by one or more theatre artists, often in collaboration with visual art, creative technologies, and other forms of performance such as music and dance. Devised theatre is often more closely related to live art (Heathfield, 2004) and performance art (Goldberg, 1988, 2004; Wark, 2006) than to traditional notions of theatre, but ultimately the maze of terminology serves devised theatre better as a metaphor in itself than as a descriptive tool. Key elements of devised theatre that differentiate it from other types of collective play creation typical in educational contexts include the commitment to multiple perspectives and subjectivities (specifically those of the creators involved), to multi-modalities (specifically lending equal weight to movement, sound, and visual technologies as opposed to the traditional dominance of text), and by extension to performances that are not led by a "sing[ular] vision," or an "authorial line" (Etchells, 1999, p. 55). The potential, then, for curriculum engagement and literacy development through devising in education comes with particular challenges and affordances that differ from other approaches to performance creation and drama in the classroom such as "playbuilding" (see Perry, Wessels, and Wager, 2013, for a detailed exploration of this).

Mia began in the autumn by introducing devising history and theory, strategies, and professional performances to a group of youth who had never directly engaged with devising practices before. During the first half of the yearlong project, interdisciplinary performance methods and non-text-based performance creation strategies were explored, followed by an engagement with spectatorship (touching on performance studies, audience studies, and performance analysis). Bringing these two processes, of creation and spectatorship, into the same space invited the connections between what and how we perform and what and how we watch and make meaning. It was on this footing that we moved into the development of a devised play for public performance.

The students came to the program with varying levels of experience in theatre and drama and varying objectives within the program. Diane, for example, was taking weekly screen acting classes outside of school, was very active in drama class, and seemed deeply invested in her various roles throughout the drama program. Nathan, on the other hand, had applied to take home economics that term, but after being excluded from that class due to numbers, he was offered drama as an alternative option. It was his first time taking drama and although he conveyed a respect for the practice, he showed little interest in doing any more than was demanded of him. Drama was offered in the school in conjunction with art; therefore those taking drama would take it for one year, and then move to art for the second year. As a result of this, some students were in the drama class solely because they wanted to take art. The various perspectives and objectives of the students in this class provided a diversity of interests and approaches within the group.

A preoccupation with its own form is a common trait of devised theatre; we wanted to explore ways for the students to be on stage, as drama students, in relation to a role that would function to expose and explore aspects of their subject positions. As the phases of work changed (from developing "tools," to watching theatre, to creating performance), so did the expectations and interactions of the students. During a group discussion, the most vocal of the students expressed their frustrations at what was perhaps a "bit too much of the abstract stuff" and a desire to get down to the real "acting" (Geraldine). Another student added: ". . . acting, to me is . . . an actor is developing a character and he throws away—he or she throws away who they are and then becomes that character" (Cassie).

The ongoing discussions around this issue revealed a significant tension between the processes we were engaged in, and the systems, structures, and models in which the youth functioned. The form of performance that was familiar and comfortable with this group was performance within a space supported by entrances and exits, props, sets, lights, costumes, curtains, and characters—a space that more clearly delineates the relationships between the performer and the performed, between the performed and the spectator, between reality and the fiction portrayed. The approach we were taking was unfamiliar territory for the students, and thus stood in the way of their expectations and assumed pathways to academic, social, and cultural objectives.

We responded to this tension by establishing a place and practice that contained enough recognizable points of contact for students to engage and invest in the work, while at the same time introducing the post-structural elements of performance practice that exist in the devising practice we were facilitating (see Perry and Rogers, 2011; Perry, Wessels, and Wager, 2013). One significant example involved the incorporation of a character development process in the devised theatre creation project. The process merged traditional acting techniques with the more experimental approaches of devising that formed the basis of the project as a whole.

Life as a Mixed Bag: Intertextual Multimodality in a Devised Theatre Project

In early spring, the students were asked to write about the their favorite genres and modalities—devices to work with in theatre. They included stories, movement, photography, and film in their responses: "stories are the best way to present meaning" (Alex); "you can make people believe things that aren't real" (Hannah); "stories are important in the lives of people, they let you become someone else" (Caitlin); "with movement you can express how you feel through your body" (Lyndsay); "music can reach people and is basically poetry one step further" (Devon); "photography, because I love the simplicity" (grade 12 participant); "film incorporates all the senses of the body" (grade 12 participant).

At this point, the students had already worked on their various scenes for the play but they felt like they wanted something to frame the emerging performance. One student, Diane, suggested:

> I think if people came on from different sides . . . [and] I could try to get a background for the screen where it's like traffic but do it in an artistic way so it's going past in a blur. I have this song that's really good, and so like each person has a different thing they're gonna do with the suitcase—someone might have something in it, someone might like drop it and everything falls out, someone might just keep going, someone might just stop in the middle and just sit there. So I was thinking it would be a good way to introduce your characters without actually saying, "hi, my name is . . ."

She then faltered, saying, "I have a vision in my mind, but I can't really describe it." The idea was then taken up by another student, Victoria, who said: "it's . . . like the idea of a street, people all going somewhere . . ." Diane corroborated: "Exactly. And if you wanted you could have the scene happen in the middle or at other times, so it could weave everything together as well."

After the discussion, Mia set up an improvisation based on this idea. The students selected music (a song by the musician Beck), and abstract visuals were projected onto a screen. For the improvisation, students took up the tools of a character and all that that entails, and a bag or container of some kind. They were asked to let go of the spoken discourse and rely on physical and gestural modalities set against the music. With these tools and adjusted hierarchy of modes, the improvisation lasted approximately ten minutes (see Figure 4.2).

In a group discussion after the improvisation, reflection, impressions, and ideas were shared. A number of students focused their reflections on the modality shift at work in the improvisation. Sam, for example, "liked how . . . you could just go

FIGURE 4.2 A clip from the bag improvisation

up to someone else's character and just have a conversation without even saying anything, you could just like with eye contact or something . . ." Kyle added: "because we couldn't talk that much . . . we had to express ourselves with our movement and our facial expressions, so while we were still our characters we were almost overdoing them so that we could get our point across whenever we interacted with someone else." These comments suggest not only the significance of the unsettling of the primacy of spoken discourse, but also the notion of play. That is, the improvisation, by loosening the structures and forms inherent in spoken language, allowed for a level of freedom in the students' explorations, interactions, and representations of the way people in our society publicly interact with one another through embodied multimodal performances.

Performing Counter Narratives

Several scenes in the performance reflect the students' use of parody and critique in their scenes. Sam, for instance, created and played the character of Princess Jaylene, adorned with ringlets and a crown and giggly, proud, and flippant. Sam imagined Jaylene as trapped in a tower in a medieval world (see Figure 4.3). Sam described the three things that kept Jaylene in the tower: she is kept there by a father who has grounded her—immediately reflective of the stereotypical teenage experience today; by her parents, who are worried that she is growing up too fast—a sentiment that she relates as true of her mom in her own life; and by a spell that can only be broken by four people finding meaning from the book that she has written about fourteen thousand things that make her happy in her tower. This last reason is related to an earlier activity in which the students incorporated various kinds of texts in their improvisations—in this case the text is an actual self-help book called *14,000 Things to Be Happy About* (Kipfer, 2007).

FIGURE 4.3 Jaylene trapped in a tower with her "happy book"

In part of the scene, after Jaylene throws her book down from the tower, Alan (in character) says, "so we just have to read it?"

JAYLENE: And find meaning.
ALAN: In your book?
GERALDINE: In a book you wrote?
JAYLENE. In my book. My dad says if I can get four people to find meaning in it I can be free.
GERALDINE (TO ALAN): She's never going to get out of that tower.

The idea of four people finding meaning in Jaylene's book was created with her group, who were at once drawing further on fairy tale conventions and at the same time parodying the real-life phenomenon of "meaning-making." In English class, Sam had hurriedly and with minimal effort written a story for an assignment; a friend of hers read it and said she didn't get it at all, but when Sam handed it in, the English teacher was full of praise, asking, "How long did that take you? There's so much meaning and depth in this." Sam and her friend were surprised and highly amused by the fact that their teacher found something so deep and meaningful in something that Sam had considered so insignificant. Sam decided to incorporate that experience into the play and, as a result, finding meaning from Sam's "happy book" became the some-what ridiculous challenge in the scene that would free her from the spell.

The interpretations, meanings, and the different ways we each experience a common thing became a common topic of exploration in the class. Often, it troubled a more familiar pattern of thought in school, where there are "right" interpretations and "wrong" ones (of information, literature, etc.). A heightened awareness of individual meaning-making processes at times became debilitating for the youth as they oscillated between the playful creation of stories and characters, and the serious (or at times facetious) exploration of subtexts, multiple perspectives, and even the merits of "randomness" in their work. This aspect of their process prompted the creation of a scene whereby a small group of students played them-selves trying to devise a scene out of the array of individual and group texts and images that had been generated over the preceding few weeks. It provided the students with a space to play ironically and satirically with the complex and yet direct and inevitable relationship between the intended and the interpreted; the self and the performed.

The extent to which Sam's character, Jaylene, wanted to be freed from the tower was not straightforward. Her own resistance to growing up, and pleasure in the "things in her tower" kept this narrative complex and unresolved. At the same time, this was just one narrative element about a character in a cast of fifteen students who were variously positioned in relation to their own characters and imagined worlds. Through these imagined selves they portrayed, in serious and playful ways, issues and narratives that were intimately and intricately connected to their lives, their experience of life so far and of life perceived around them.

Sam's tower scene resonates with some of the issues and narratives portrayed in the clinic scene described in the opening vignette. The tower scene is in part a critique of the confined female adolescent body told through a fairy tale genre, and part resistance to that narrative. In another part of the clinic scene described above, the characters explored resistance as represented by the tattooed female body, creating a resonance with some of the zine pages described in Chapter 2. In this section of the clinic scene, Roxy, a tattoo artist, connected with Lexa, who was also an artist and had tattoos on her body:

ROXY: I saw your sketches. What do you do?
LEXA: Actually I sculpt. You?
ROXY: I'm a tattoo artist.
LEXA: Oh, cool, I have a couple of tats myself. What are you in for?

Soon after this exposition, Emma (the receptionist) approached Roxy to ask if she would make her an appointment to get a tattoo.

ANNIE: So, I heard you are a tattoo artist?
ROXY: That's right.
EMMA: Do you think you could, maybe, fit me in sometime?

In this series of interactions, the characters shared experience and subjectivities, rather than attempting to monitor or challenge themselves. Art, throughout this scene, functioned as a coalescing engagement—Lexa is a sculptor and sketches in a notebook while she waits for her appointment, which prompts the interest and inquiries of Roxy. In the case of tattoo art, the body becomes art as well as implicated through art. The tattooed body here was set against the body as a subject of testing, offering a counterpoint or counter discourse to the medicalizing and surveillance discourse of the urban feminine body in the majority of the scene (Grosz, 1994). Lexa, in her biographical statement, had listed "artist" as a descriptor and associated her creativity with drug-induced inspiration, lamenting the perceived binary of medicalization/creativity. In this scene, the tattoo, and occupation of tattoo artist, became another visible, performative, and embodied representation of transgressive behaviors. In the broader discourses of urban youth culture, including those at the zine site described in Chapter 2, tattoos function as signs literally inscribed on bodies as markers of resistance, both physical and cultural.

Immediately preceding the clinic scene in the final performance, April performed a monologue in the role of her character, Lexa. In the background there was a drawing of a large clock displayed on the wall. She began by pulling a clock off the side of the stage and said, "Sometimes I want to smash this thing . . . just looking at these numbers makes me crazy. Each heavy hour is draining my freedom [sits down on floor]. Now it's so limiting and controlled, unlike my life before . . ." In the scene, Lexa contrasted this life with her previous "chaotic life" that included the freedom to do "whatever, whenever"—a life that also included illegal drugs and a successful art career (see Figures 4.4 and 4.5). The monologue portrayed her circumstances of rehabilitation, medical dependence, and a highly structured day-to-day life, emphasizing the inevitability and predictability of what will make up the rest of her days. In these performances of Lexa, April provided an example of how the performance space allowed the students to create a character that incorporates both lived and perceived realities and to create hybridized and interrelated positions from which to perform counter narratives.

FIGURE 4.4 Clip 1, April performing her monologue as Lexa

FIGURE 4.5 Clip 2, April performing her monologue as Lexa

In reflecting on her performances, April said, "It all started out 'cause I wanted to be a little bit older than our age right now." She articulated the interrelations between her understandings of herself and her character in this way: "The creative side of Lexa, my character, was based upon me . . . [but] her personal experiences, I've obviously not really had." It is these experiences that point to "the raw parts of life that aren't so great," and that became central to her character biography. In identifying with the character, April said: "She's obviously having a down time and, you know, everyone's kind of had that." April sometimes went "people watching" downtown, exploring parts of the city usually cut off from her day-to-day life; she referred to this experience as influential, and one that affected her work in the character development process. She explained:

> [My cousin] does acting, too, and he was talking about some personal experiences or—from his friends that he put in and I don't know, I just kind of like referenced to that 'cause he lives, I guess, more in Downtown Vancouver and he sees a lot more of, you know, kind of raw parts of life that aren't so great. But—and yeah, and he always talks about, like, just walking around there and seeing things. And I actually went to go see myself a few times with a friend 'cause we went to Downtown Vancouver twice. And, yeah, it was really interesting people watching and you can just see a lot of stuff and you just kind of absorb it. And when I think about people with issues and, like, to make my character, actually, kind of like what are the issues that I see around and stuff. And I just kind of absorbed that and put it in—yeah.

In reflecting specifically on her monologue in the final interview, April focused on the conscious imagining of an adult life based on things she sees and hears—a life that is stressful and dictated by time until faced with a crisis.

APRIL: I don't know, I would just kind of read certain things and, like, oh, that's really good or just kind of hear things subconsciously that people say or, like, little lines—everyday kinds of things, and I don't know it just kind of all came together.
THERESA: It seemed like you were kind of in a way taking on the perspective of a more adult person.
APRIL: Yeah, I was more so.
THERESA: You know, dealing with overscheduled lives, is that what you kind of imagined?
APRIL: Yeah. Like, and a person who's under the stress of change. Like, intense change. Like, all of a sudden just stop, drop everything and do this. Actually the last line, "Only time can tell," came from a song. I just kind of added it at the end. I'm, like, whoa, that's ironic.

It became apparent, through the characters created and represented in the clinic scenes and the monologue, that the students troubled the perceived distinctions between what is normal and what is transgressive, and constructed urban feminine subjectivity in ways that were at times representative of stereotypes, but at other times were complex and contradictory portrayals. The devised theatre process provided a context within which these girls could create a represented private/public space (a clinic) to explore particular discourses of urban feminine subjectivity at the interstices between lived experience and the imagined self. These discourses are necessarily partial and conflicting as the urban, and in particular the Downtown Eastside, became a kind of text for their performances. We would also argue that the performed discourses and characters in the clinic scene clearly pushed boundaries of acceptability or expected activity as understood by the students involved. Throughout the creation process, this space pushed against an implicit surveillance role of the anticipated audience of parents and teachers.

In similar ways, the other performers created characters that combined aspects of their lived and imagined selves. In these creative spaces of character development processes, scene creation, and performances, students were able to alter and expand their experiences (lived, imagined, performed) as urban youth. They drew on these resources in playful, parodic, and serious ways to interrogate their own lives, the lives of imagined others, and to critique larger discourses and societal structures that they had encountered so far.

Talking Back: Performing Adolescence in a Public Space

The two public productions took place in the theatre space at Lismore Secondary School in early May. The performance was described in the program this way:

> This performance has grown out of a collaborative creation process that we call devising. Over the past four months the grade nine drama class has been exploring ideas, characters, media and movement. The piece of work that we are presenting tonight does not represent any single artistic or authorial vision, rather it is a presentation of multiple ideas, themes, characters and ambitions. A princess is trapped in a tower with a list of things that make her happy; a group of students try to be productive and creative under the pressure of time and making meaning; and characters and creators collide on streets, in clinics and in bars. We hope that through the many perspectives and personalities that have created this piece we will allow you to continue the process by bringing your own.

The students' preferred name for the performance was *Life, the Universe and Nothing in Particular*, though in the end the teacher selected a different title. The play lasted approximately forty-five minutes and all cast members were on the stage throughout the performance, with the exception of people leaving to take off and bring on props and set pieces. The stage was backed by a large projection screen, onto which students projected images generated during the creation process or using the shadow screen. These images included drawings of flowers, desks, and clocks, photographs of piano keys and no exit signs, and students acting as band members behind the shadow screen (for a bar scene). Recorded music, including songs by Beck, the Swell Season, and the Beatles (e.g., "Let It Be"), was used during transitions and movement pieces. Lighting was designed and operated by two grade 12 students with the help of the drama teacher and a colleague from the University of British Columbia.

The performance revolved around four main scenes. Interwoven with these scenes were monologues and movement sequences. The play therefore didn't portray a continual story line, or represent consistent themes or topics. Rather, it could be better described as a collage of ideas and processes. The "tower scene" revolved around a princess trying to break the curse of her father that keeps her there by finding four people who will read her book of "things to be happy about" and find meaning in it. The "clinic scene" was a portrayal of four young women dealing with various transgressive circumstances including unwanted pregnancy, drug abuse, and promiscuity. The "bar scene" involved a group of aspiring musicians battling with the confidence and the means to pursue their dreams. The "process scene" was the anomalous scene inasmuch as it involved the cast members abandoning their characters and adopting the roles of drama students under pressure to create a performance. The monologues were developed exposés of two particular characters from the play. Finally, the movement sequences were places in which these divergent worlds and characters collided with one another, always accompanied by a material or metaphorical representation of the "luggage" of their lives.

Victoria explained in her interview:

> Some of the characters didn't come from us but I think, like, what issues in life they dealt with like, drugs. We've seen a lot of things on TV and then people talking to us about that or just, like, this other kind of life that we hear about, which we think is powerful because of the different track that people go through in life that we didn't get to experience. So we're seeing them through [their] eyes. . . . And I think this performance was really interesting for me because I got to express something that was powerful . . . just the fact that you can share something that everyone understands or may not understand. Or just the fact that you get to share something and be part of, like, the performance.

After each performance, Mia facilitated a talk-back session with the audience. During these sessions, the students took on the role of "experts" of their work, of their role as actors and creators, and of their experience as students, teenagers, and social critics. A sample of a talk-back exchange follows:

MIA (TO AUDIENCE): If you all have time, say another ten or fifteen minutes, we are having a talk-back session. This is a process-based piece so it calls for some discussion. Does anyone have a question for the students?

YOUNG AUDIENCE MEMBER: In the first half of the play there is a girl carrying a heavy bucket around. Why were you doing that?

VICTORIA: Okay, there are all these representation things. The empty bucket I carry is kind of like the baggage I have to carry. It's heavy for me but for other people it's empty.

AUDIENCE MEMBER: How did you come up with the whole thing?

KYLE: Well we came up with scenes and all the scenes are representing our characters, the things we carry around with us every day. We used the bags as like a transition between scenes that don't really make sense together.

SAME AUDIENCE MEMBER: Would it be the same performance on another night?

STUDENTS (ALL TALK LOUDLY AT ONCE AND LAUGH, MOST OF THE TALK IS INAUDIBLE): Maybe! Sort of!

Audience members also asked about whether the students considered foregoing the stage/audience tradition all together. Some students said they had considered it and pointed to times when they included the audience when handing out candy and flowers during the tower scene. Mia pointed out that the whole process was already quite experimental and the students had taken many risks already so they kept some of the conventions. Throughout the talk-back session, individual students provided more information on what inspired their characters and scenes, such as a poem they had written or having the desire to be a singer but not knowing how to go about becoming one. In the talk-back and the performance itself, the students demonstrated how they used "the power of theatre to . . . re-imagine themselves in all their complexity" (Gallager, 2011, p. 154).

Devised theatre as taken up with youth at this site afforded an open engagement with relationships and subjectivities, always contingent upon location and context. The central role of subjectivity and interrelationality in this devising work rendered the representations partial and approximate. Susan said in her final interview: "It can mean everything and anything to anybody else."

The significance of the urban imaginary in the students' work and performance did not come about due to an interest imposed by a teacher or researcher. Rather, the locations, themes, and discourses emerged as students addressed and explored their own subjectivities and positions (Gallagher, 2007). The final performances emerged as a complex representation of space, location, and subjectivities in relation to peers, parents, teachers, and institutional contexts.

Although the time frame of the public aspect of the project at this site was more finite, in many instances during the year the youth engaged in various forms of public resistance—to the school structures, to this form of theatre, to the larger societal discourses they sometimes incorporated into their work. As in the other sites, these resistances were fluid and unfixed, yet provide evidence that the students were present civic actors in their lives (Ginwright, Noguerra, and Cammarota, 2006).

In the next and final chapter of this book, we further theorize the relationship between the performative work of the youth at this site, as well as the zine and anti-violence site, and the implications for understanding the interplay of the arts, media, and critical literacies among youth, public pedagogy, and the intersections of local and global participation in democratic citizenship.

References

Etchells, T. (1999). *Certain fragments: Contemporary performance and forced entertainment.* London: Routledge.

Gallagher, K. (2007). *The theatre of urban: Youth and schooling in dangerous times.* Toronto: University of Toronto Press.

Gallagher, K. (2011). Editorial: Drama and theatre in urban contexts. *RIDE: The Journal of Applied Theatre and Performance, 16*(2), 151–156.

Ginwright, S., Noguerra, P., & Cammarota, J. (2006). *Beyond resistance! Youth activism and community change.* New York: Routledge.

Goldberg, R. (1988). *Performance art: From futurism to the present.* London: Thames and Hudson.

Goldberg, R. (2004). *Performance: Live art since the 60s.* New York: Thames and Hudson.

Grosz, E. (1994). *Volatile bodies: Toward a corporeal feminism.* Bloomington: Indiana University Press.

Haraway, D. (1983). The ironic dream of a common language for women in the integrated circuit: Science, technology, and socialist feminism in the 1980s or a socialist feminist manifesto for cyborgs. *History of Consciousness Board.* University of California at Santa Cruz. Retrieved from http://www.egs.edu/faculty/donna-haraway/articles/donna-haraway-the-ironic-dream-of-a-common-language-for-women-in-the-integrated-circuit/

Heathfield, A. (2004). *LIVE: Art and performance.* New York: Routledge.

Kipfer, B. A. (2007). *14,000 things to be happy about.* New York: Workman Publishing.

Perry, M., & Rogers, T. (2011). Meddling with "drama class," muddling "urban": Imagining aspects of the urban feminine self through an experimental theatre process with youth. *Research in Drama Education: The Journal of Applied Theatre and Performance, 16*(2), 197–213.

Perry, M., Wessels, A., & Wager, A. C. (2013). From playbuilding to devising in literacy education: Aesthetic and pedagogical approaches. *Journal of Adolescent and Adult Literacy, 56*(8), 649–658.

Wark, J. (2006). *Radical gestures: Feminism and performance art in North America.* Montreal: McGill-Queens University Press.

5

YOUTH CLAIMS IN A GLOBAL CITY

Texts, Discourses, and Spaces of Youth Literacies

> Street people are interested in writing, art and shit like that . . . I want to read and write better to give myself a kick in the ass. I don't care what the reaction is as long as it's a reaction.
>
> *Jordan*

We set out to support the arts, media, and critical literacy practices among youth in diverse community and school settings in one city as they spoke to and interacted with local and more global publics. The youth we worked with in this project demonstrated that they are sophisticated critical and cultural theorists and important and vocal participants in local and global conversations about contemporary social issues, collective democratic life, and social justice. As the title of our project (YouthCLAIM) suggests, youth in this city, as elsewhere, are using various forms of art, media, and literacy to make an alternative set of truth claims about their lives and social worlds—counter narratives that interrupt larger cultural discourses, particularly many of the common discourses of homelessness, violence, and adolescence. They draw on a rich mix of discursive resources and critical practices to make these claims. We wanted to capture and document the claims they made, and the kind of multimodal intertextual processes they engaged in while writing, drawing, filming, and performing, as well as how this work constitutes critical arts, media, and literacy production in communities and a school in one urban location.

We begin our conclusion by locating this work in a conceptualization of the cultural spaces of the youth as they engaged with, re-imagined, and resisted received narratives about their lives and social worlds. To fully appraise the reach of their productions and claims, we explore the implications of their various public sites of address. We theorize their work as critical literacy practices, as forms of engaged, public and, at times, radical pedagogy, and as forms of civic engagement. Their local productions offer alternative views as set against corporate globalized and popular culture. We close this final chapter with a call for significantly rethinking and broadening our formal or schooled approaches to arts, media, and critical literacy practices among youth.

Youth in the Cultural Spaces of a Global City

This project was located in Vancouver, Canada, in the years leading up to the 2010 Olympics. The world gaze was turned toward Vancouver as an emerging global city and it revealed contradictory visions. It was represented as a prosperous and livable city, while also containing a dark underbelly of poverty, homelessness, and addiction—contradictions the youth were fully aware of and lived themselves. The script of a story from *Dan Rather Reports* (2011), shot just before the Olympics, reads:

> The city of Vancouver boasts that it is one of the richest cities in North America . . . and is repeatedly voted the most livable city in the world . . . but visit . . . the Dickensian underside of the city, the so-called Downtown Eastside, and it's a different story. . . . Tourists who take a wrong turn off the cobblestoned downtown streets are likely to find used syringes laying on the sidewalks, streets lined with homeless people, prostitutes making their rounds, and junkies shooting up in broad daylight.

The visual images that accompany the script shift from buildings set against beautiful sea and mountain skylines to impoverished-looking people and drug users in the Downtown Eastside of Vancouver (see Figures 5.1 and 5.2).

To fully scrutinize and appreciate the work the youth created within this context, we view it as both deeply local and also inflected with wider national and international or global influences and discourses. We recognize that contemporary youth literacy practices often sit at the intersections of the local and the global in terms of the flows and exchange of information, knowledge, new media, etc.—what Appadurai (1996) refers to as "scapes" (e.g., ideoscapes, mediascapes). These intersections and disjunctures of the local and global scapes result in the creation of an urban imaginary with particular kinds of discourses and productions among the youth in this city. To explore the practices of the youth in these three sites—their use of discursive resources of embodied subjectivity, arts, media, and literacies—we look at what they produced through this spatial lens.

Jordan, whose work we described in Chapter 2, speaks from the margins of contemporary urban life. He improvised a popular and persuasive art object, a multimodal poster using verbal and visual resources that speaks back to the moral injustice of leaving rigs (used heroin needles) in a children's park and which he

FIGURE 5.1 Image of the DTES

Credit: http://commons.wikimedia.org/wiki/File:DTES_Alley_Culture.jpg

FIGURE 5.2 Image of city of Vancouver

Credit: http://en.wikipedia.org/wiki/Architecture_of_Vancouver

imagined inserting into a public space. As cultural objects, posters have evolved more into artistic rather than political statements in capitalist society; however, there is a history of their role as radical political signs and revolutionary art in other times and contexts (Sontag, 1999); they remain a tactic among activists around the globe, and are experiencing a new life in digital contexts as signs in selfies. Jordan's sophisticated appropriation of this form, though complicated in terms of a shifting audience (other street youth, drug users, and in some sense the program coordinators who painted over a mural that his friend had painted), nonetheless created an improvised and effective cultural counter narrative.

When Kaity articulated a plan for creating a film that captures pre-Olympic Vancouver as a moment in time, she realized that her narrative is set against a changing landscape in a shifting geography of place: "The city's losing a lot of character and I want to capture it before it changes and shatters into pieces." As we argued in Chapter 3, Kaity's film description can be seen as a form of narrative testimonial of a contemporary urban imaginary that focuses on the variety of embodied and spatialized youth (busking in the streets, smoking pot at the art gallery lawn, hanging out in Kits, sleeping on buses) who would soon be displaced. Youth like Kaity residing in these local spaces, much like the artists of San Francisco described in *Hollow City* (Solnit and Schwartzenberg, 2000), often serve as barometers of this loss of artistic, political, spiritual, and social life of the city.

In the school performance project described in Chapter 4, a group of young women imagined a scene in a health clinic for women older than themselves that revealed a sophisticated understanding of the normative public discourses about the female body that circulate locally and more globally. They engaged in a risky process of exploring and representing aspects of themselves in relation to experienced and imagined stories that are slightly removed yet proximal to their own. In doing so, they reinscribed and remapped their own lived and embodied subjectivities, resisting the limitations of what is considered appropriate discourse in school contexts.

In this spatial context, the contemporary urban city at particular moments in time, the youth created these multimodal productions to make material and cultural claims about their lives and social worlds. A poster about rigs at least momentarily claims attention for an injustice; an imagined film about a city in the midst of gentrification makes claims about the loss of the cultural life; a film about teenage stereotypes resists particular figurations of youth while risking re-inscription in an ongoing process of circulating narratives; and an imagined women's clinic scene makes visible gendered lives by calling on the present and imagined futures in a proximal urban space.

Multimodal Intertextuality as Identity Work and Resources of Critique

The youth claims in this project achieve power through multimodal intertextuality—the mix of genres, forms, and modes that functioned as discursive resources for creating counter narratives—to comment on their material conditions and lived experiences. Across the three sites, the youth exploited genre forms, modes, and practices in their work, juxtaposing and hybridizing and remixing these cultural forms, from reversing messages in corporate ads and playfully using public service announcement genres to performing revised fairy tales. They took up these flexible cultural forms, genres that continually circulate in a network of relations of power and dialogue, to bridge or minimize gaps between discourses and produce new and often playful or powerful forms of expression.

Their claims can also be seen as a kind of identity work. The youth positioned and repositioned their own subjectivities in and through their productions (Davies and Harre, 1990; Holland et al., 1998). In much of their work, the body is referenced, contributing to the creation and representations of lived realities and continually inscribed with, and generating information about, youth subjectivity and positioning (Grosz, 1994; Grosz and Eisenman, 2001). In her identity video, *traceiisawesome*, for instance, Tracei positions herself as a young woman through the literal embodiment of expression and resistance to the cultural narratives of femininity. Through piercing and cross-dressing images, she creates a kind of parody of gender identity, using words and the genre of the public service announcement to send home the message. As we argued in Chapter 3, this multimodal intertextuality of media and digital resources is a particularly productive space for appropriating, refiguring, and imagining new embodiments. As did many of her peers in this project, Tracei appropriated the discursive resources of embodiment, texts and cultural stereotypes to talk back to dominant cultural narratives of her life and her social worlds.

In other examples of performative embodied positioning, Max, in creating scenes for the film of teenage stereotypes (Chapter 3), is acutely aware of the way his body can be seen as an object of desire and his performance parodies this in the film with exaggerated gestures and monologue; April, performing as the character "Lexa" (Chapter 4), embodies a woman slightly older, a female urban subject open to scrutiny based on reproductive choices. In her performance, she reproduces normative societal discourses and reveals a critical awareness of the ways that the female body is monitored and regulated and a subject of public scrutiny.

The Critical Tools of Satire: Irony and Parody

We were particularly and continually interested in and compelled by the sophisticated use of parody and satire across the three sites as the youth took on these complex societal issues. Parody and satire often include poached texts and new media, operating as oppositional tactics used to create new texts—this recombination works to both unsettle and reassert cultural discourses. Parody was created when the youth were simultaneously oriented toward a subject, and to how that subject or topic is addressed by others through language or image—that is, they created a text about text. These satires were created through language, image, sound, and body.

Jae's appropriation of the MasterCard ad in Chapter 2 forcefully illustrates the power of poaching and transforming cultural materials. The productive tension of parody is situated at the intersection of fidelity to the original and improvisation. In Jae's version there is a pointed contrast between those who live on the margins of society and the assumed audience of the original ad. The remixed ad repositions Jae as someone who effectively speaks back to power through using parody as a counter narrative strategy.

The conflicting social values that are revealed through satire are also clearly represented in Fraggle's poem titled "The truth (hurts)" (Mills and Rogers, 2009). Using an ironic tone, Fraggle turns the discourses of yuppie/poverty dichotomy on its head. The poem is constructed by depicting street people as stronger, freer, and more real than yuppies—"when it all comes crashing down / i will be the one to take your hand / tell you that there is life beyond your line of credit"—yet ultimately no different. The poem becomes a powerful counter narrative to common discourses of homeless youth heard on the street and in the media, particularly at a time when the city was increasingly policing the homeless, as well as to larger cultural narratives of capitalism and consumerism.

Sam, in her revised fairy tale performance (Chapter 4), takes on the embodied subjectivity of an overprotected daughter who is stuck in a tower. The only way she can be released is if others find meaning in a book that defies meaningful interpretation. This scene was based on group input during the process of improvising; however, it also emanated out of earlier discussions about the role of devised theatre to draw on conventions of story and interpretation in order to parody both the fairy tale form and the act of meaning-making itself.

As we argued in Chapter 2, parody and satire can be seen as tactical uses of text and media that are likely to be localized inventions of practices that contest dominant values and discourses, as opposed to "strategic" uses of media that uphold or perpetuate them (DeCerteau, 1984). As other researchers and scholars in the areas of literacy and media have observed, citizens on the margins of society often engage in similar tactical uses of public spaces—borrowing, poaching, and recombining popular culture texts for their own ends (Boler, 2008; Knobel and Lankshear, 2002; Jocson, 2013). The use of irony, parody, and satire among youth at the three sites in this project reflects these tactics and strengthens their claims about homelessness, violence, and contemporary adolescent bodies and experiences— producing lively counter narratives to dominant cultural discourses.

Publics and Public Pedagogy: Complex Sites of Address

Engaging with youth across these diverse sites in one urban area allowed us to witness the ways they took up public sites of address for their work. Drawing once again on the work of Bakhtin, we argue that texts are fundamentally dialogic, always addressing others, and in many ways unfinished. The sites of address of the youth in the project were varied. Some of their productions were addressed to very local publics as in the original paper version of the zine written primarily for other street-involved youth (see Figure 5.3). Some productions were addressed to larger

FIGURE 5.3 Anniversary edition of zine

live publics, such as the poetry anthology and launch (see Figure 5.5), the yearly celebration of the arts program at the center for street youth, the outreach work of the youth at the LOVE site, and the theatre performance of the Lismore students (see Figures 5.7 and 5.8). Yet other productions became part of larger networked publics, including some of the videos on homelessness (see Figure 5.4), the LOVE project videos (see Figure 5.6), and the street youth webzine, Anotherslice.ca.

In making these claims about their lives and social worlds, youth implicitly and explicitly questioned the kind of place their city is or was—the marginalization of particular populations, the responsibilities of urban dwellers, how the city interacts

FIGURE 5.4 Link to videos about homelessness

FIGURE 5.5 Poster for poetry anthology book launch

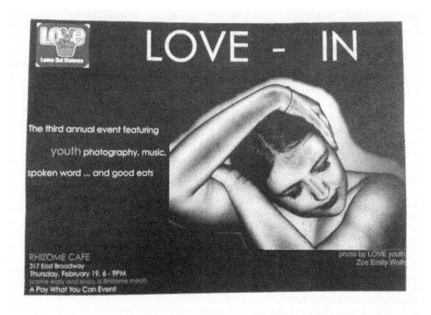

FIGURE 5.6 Poster for LOVE fundraising event

FIGURE 5.7 Poster for Lismore performance

FIGURE 5.8 Lismore students participating in the talk-back after the performance

with other places, and the consequences for ongoing social justice projects. Given the ways neoliberal forces are variously reconfiguring urban environments locally and globally through privatization, unregulated markets, commercialization of culture, gentrification, and rescaling to a global economy, youth collectively engaged in the process of asking what alternatives, large and small, might be imagined for themselves and for others. They did this work through critical literacy practices, particularly through identity work, engaging with tactics of parody, satire and counter narrative, and by addressing particular kinds of publics.

We argue that these public pedagogies are relational to the alternative, multiple, counterpublics that they address (Fraser, 1993; Warner, 2002), small and large, that create new forms and sites of public engagement. As Fraser (1993) argues in revising Habermas's notion of the public sphere, in any socially and economically stratified society there exists the need for multiple, competing, and sometimes contesting publics in order to expand democratic discursive spaces. These publics have been variously referred to as, for instance, "counterpublics" (Fraser, 1990; Warner, 2002) and/or "little publics" (Hickey-Moody, 2013, p. 19).

The idea of a counterpublic or a little public can take the form of particular concrete audiences, or audiences to texts that circulate and recirculate in ongoing conversations. Counterpublics, in particular, often assume a power difference between the members and the larger public as in the case of youth culture broadly understood and marginalized youth in particular. The productions of youth in these contexts are often what Hickey-Moody (2013) describes as vernacular—they are not so much about the arts, media, or literacy product itself as they are social commentaries on everyday lives. In addressing publics, these productions teach specific ideas about young people to their audiences that can be understood as a form of citizenship. The audiences that were drawn together to view the aesthetic work of youth in these sites contributed to the possibilities for civic engagement that connect experience, institutions, and critical exchange. In this digital era, it is particularly essential to recognize the importance of live audiences and to view these publics and counterpublics as modes of community attachment that have the potential to actively contribute to debates about the public good.

We argue that, collectively, the youth we worked with were saying important things to their respective communities and audiences and to larger publics about social issues in their lives, about the growing material inequities of their contemporary global city, and about new forms of youth identifications (Dillabough and Kennelly, 2010; Talburt and Lesko, 2014). This occurred when a young man living on the streets, Marcin, directly addressed social workers in his community, admonishing them for treating street youth as victims, and when Steven addressed the limitations of the policies related to programs for homeless youth in his film. It occurred when the youth at LOVE told their stories to younger students in schools and created a "youth-oriented" film to celebrate their history of anti-violence outreach work in the community over seven years. And it occurred when a group of students in a secondary school performed a scene about the difficult knowledge of the lives of women who have dealt with unwanted pregnancy and drug addiction in their proximal urban center. In all of these cases, the youth took risks in speaking back to live, local, and larger publics. In some ways these forms of public pedagogy begin to reach toward radical pedagogical possibilities (e.g., Anyon, 2014); that is, the youth productions are critical, political, and public pedagogical work—work that is oriented toward social critique and social change.

Indeed, the ways the youth addressed these smaller and larger publics in this project through their arts, media, and literacy practices and productions constitute the multiple forms of public pedagogy in the lives of young people (Giroux, 2000; Sandlin, Schultz, and Burdick, 2010). Public pedagogy is an important site of investigation among other feminist and critical theorists for examining the kinds of learning that occurs outside the boundaries of schools and state sanctioned curricula that inhabits "complex and ambiguous spaces of pedagogical address" (Ellsworth, 2005; Sandlin, O'Malley, and Burdick, 2011, p. 3). Our work with the youth in this project directly addresses such complex and ambiguous spaces of learning. This project took us from the street to the community center to the classroom, and on- and off-line, in seeking to support and engage with youth who were, through literacy, arts, and media, creatively and critically constructing counter narratives to normative cultural discourses and making public and critical claims about their bodies, lives, city, and society.

The youth in this project took on issues of common interest, or what should be common interest issues, for the betterment of society. These issues included, for instance: mobilizing more integrated and responsive services for street youth; recognizing all the places in which violence resides, including private spaces, and speaking back to it in public forums such as schools and community centers; and creating opportunities to imaginatively engage with civic issues within curricular spaces. The youth were often explicit about this aspect of their work, as in Jordan's opening quote about getting a reaction, as well as by other youth across the project. As Kaity said about her films in the LOVE site: "Sharing your films or just speaking out is sometimes enough to let other people in; speaking it is living it." And Amy, at the end of the Lismore performance, said, "[Our scene in the play just meant] here's a group of all these people in a [clinic] . . . and all of them have problems that a lot of people have . . . and some people can handle it and some people can't . . . showing that these are real problems that the world has at the moment."

Their public pedagogy occupied both embodied places and digital spaces— through publishing paper and online versions of the zine, a poetry chapbook, and films about youth homelessness, through speaking about violence in schools, and creating and sharing digital videos about youth and anti-violence in a public forum, and also through the creation of an original theatre performance for a local school community. Together with perspectives on informal learning (e.g., Bekerman, Burbules, and Silberman-Keller, 2007), this framework has the potential to transform our understanding of theory and practice that includes a more profound connection between education and public life.

From Public Pedagogies to Local and Global Civic Engagement

In thinking about these youth productions, we can examine intersections of the local and the global in contemporary forms of cultural participation by drawing on current discussions of media literacy, post-structural feminist theories, critical perspectives, and the work of cultural geographers. According to Jenkins et al. (2006), youth participatory culture includes producing and circulating content that results in a kind of "convergence culture." Claims are made that this convergence culture has the potential to repair the damage caused by an increasing privatized culture (Jenkins et al., 2006, p. 256) or, as we argue, to offer alternatives to widely circulating and often corporatized forms of popular culture.

When we examine learning more broadly to take into account a variety of public spheres, we can begin to connect the larger culture, the productions of youth, and the challenges of radical democracy in a newly constituted global public. In his theorization of public pedagogy, Giroux (2005) seeks to position "public bodies against corporate power, connect classrooms to the challenges faced by social movements in the streets, and provide spaces within classrooms for personal injury and private terrors to be translated into public considerations and struggles" (p. 10). Because this theorization is characteristically audacious, in our own work we are careful not to overemphasize the agentive qualities and civic engagements celebrated at the intersection of youth, new literacies, and public engagement, particularly when we risk locating the primary responsibility for fomenting social change with youth (e.g., Poyntz, 2008), rather than holding a larger public and society— those they address—at least as responsible for advancing social justice.

We are also not forwarding a notion of youth as neoliberal citizens in the making; that is youth as becoming workers and consumers in a global economy in a manner that is exclusionary and decoupled from human rights (Harris, 2012). What we mean by citizenship is based on notions of democracy, dialogue, and plurality based on the work of philosophers such as Habermas, Arendt, and Dewey (e.g., Dillabough and Kennelly, 2010; Kennelly, 2006). This model of citizenship does not leave out people based on their ethnicity, gender, class, sexuality, or because they are homeless, victims of violence, or young. What we do argue is that there are spaces in which the self-expression of youth through arts, media, and literacy practices come in to contact with larger social and political discourses and structures, sometimes challenging and refuting power structures.

There were times when the youth's connection to civic engagement was more vague and tenuous. For instance, Tracei felt the public was generally oblivious and once they read or viewed some of their work they might say, "Oh, I get it." Others described a mix of civic engagement goals and personal goals. One youth (Tweek) at the zine site talked about the importance of social consciousness and responsibility (citing "Dr. King"), but also said writing something helped pay the rent. Others railed against being stereotyped, and wanted audiences to both laugh (e.g., at the *Teenage Kicks* film) but also, as Max said, "to take it seriously." And the students in the theatre performance were eager to explore new subject positions in order to express their own understanding of social issues.

Others were more impassioned about their civic engagement. Although Jae was surprised when Jordan even submitted to the zine while we were there ("He's a bad-ass and not as educated as I am"), Jordan had clear and informed critical views that he expressed in various ways. As he said in his interview, "I'm a pretty outspoken person, anything I can argue a point for." When asked what he likes to read, he said the street zines were important to him and that "so many cities have them [but] a lot are [just] one or two issues and disappear. In Vancouver there are so many homeless here so it lasts." He continued to discuss the then current challenges to his lifestyle as a committed street-involved person: "The Olympics has caused nothing but problems—more cops who beat people up. In Georgia [site of 1994 Olympics] they got rid of homeless kids or put them in jail . . . it's a homeless paradise [here] except the cops." In this interview, Jordan analyzed his city and its laws, such as the "Safe Streets Act" that made panhandling and related activities illegal and concomitant brutality of police in enforcing it. He moves seamlessly between this analysis and a recollection of similar police responses more than a decade earlier in another North American city to make his claims. Kaity also had a clear vision of the urban political landscape and believed youth needed to "take the bull by the horns" in speaking up about social policy issues related to housing, poverty, the environment, and drugs: as she said, "speaking it is living it."

In looking closely at what youth say and do in this one urban location, and in relation to smaller and larger audiences, we begin to understand the potential circulation of ideas or cultural motion at the intersection of local and more global discourses. In this way, the way the local constituted with echoes of more global discourses; that is, the local is continually "contaminated" by the global (Bhabha, 1996, p. 54), and any understanding of the global is not conceivable without attention to how discourses and practices are produced/reproduced in the local (Massey, 2007). Appadurai (1996) discusses the way locality is produced and reproduced in relation to contemporary urban life against the backdrop of national regimes that produce compliant citizens, mass mediation, and commodification. He defines this process of locality as always emergent and fragile, and as a kind of translocal struggle that includes the subversions and resistances of citizens in everyday lives who are at odds with the project of nationhood.

In many ways the youth in this project were at odds with the nationhood project. The street youth were constantly speaking back to the discourses about homeless people, the policies that impinged on their lives, the misdirected services, and societal inequities. The LOVE youth were engaged in a transnational project that speaks back to the structures that result in violence in homes and communities. The Lismore students, located as they were in a school site, pushed back against normalizing cultural discourses of gender and youth that limit adolescent subjectivities.

We can view civic engagement at least in part through the perspective of resistance. Particularly for youth, and for youth at the margins of urban life, civic engagement may take the form of resisting regulation of their bodies and movements, or contesting inequities and dominant cultural narratives. Whether or not youth view their work as civic engagement or resistance work, as Soep (2012) argues, we need to understand the gray areas between their actions, intentions, and the social implications of their work. As Michelle Fine so eloquently states: "Resistance is an epistemology, a line of vision, theorizing and analysis: it does not require intent and it does not guarantee victory, it simply presumes a human yearning for dignity and action . . . youth like the rest of us, speak in marbleized tongues, braiding discursive currents of critique and fear, desire and ambivalence . . ." (Fine, Tuck, and Yang, 2014, pp. 49–50). These perspectives on resistance are generous in relation to the possibility that youth will find meaning as their public pedagogies and civic engagements, often momentary and partial and at other times more sustained and committed, unfold in time and in the context of institutional histories, urban contexts, and particular nation-states, and also in retrospect; that is youth resistance and engagement can be viewed as continually contingent rather than fixed.

As we have argued elsewhere (Rogers et al., 2014), it is important to recognize the contradictions and complexities of these engagements, particularly when youth might be understood as living with precarity (Butler, 2009)—a condition in which certain populations suffer from failing social and economic networks of support. Precarious subjects struggle to be legible and recognizable within established societal norms. The project and the work we have described in this book represent the complex and discursive participation of youth in civic life. Youth here are engaging, reproducing and resisting larger societal and cultural discourses as they seek to make themselves, as precarious subjects, more legible and recognizable public citizens in the face of broken promises of democracy. In these ways, we can view their practices as both constituting and, at times, restructuring the social and cultural life of a contemporary global or world city.

Youth, Critical Literacies, and Civic Engagement: Implications for Schooling

We initially proposed and embarked on this project in a time when it was becoming increasingly evident that adolescents were engaging with and negotiating of a broad range of genres and text forms in and out of schools, becoming skilled and flexible communicators across a range of print and non-print media (e.g., Alvermann, 2002; Luke and Elkins, 1998); and there were increasing calls for new instructional practices (e.g., New London Group, 1996). Based on our own work and the work of many educators involved with youth arts and media, we broaden that call for creating classroom places in which these rich youth literacy practices are integrated into the curricula in ways that preserve the creativity and power to reconstruct the dominant stories around them. Curricular spaces can be created in schools that either open up or close down the possibilities for engaging adolescents, depending on the beliefs, methodologies, and practices that are constructed (Rogers, 2000). At a time when there are increasing calls for common curricula, we want to make a case here, instead, for an uncommon curriculum in schools—one in which adolescents are engaging with the tools and processes of arts, media, and critical literacy practices in sophisticated ways in order to engage with and interrogate the world around them.

Art, media, and critical literacy practices provide a site for youth to represent complex, fluid, and shifting discursive and embodied subject positions, and to participate in the civic engagement. Analysis of the work of the youth in these sites reveals these positionings through juxtapositions of body, text, image, and sound created at the intersection of writing, creating, performing, and filming while interacting with and engaging with larger and smaller publics. The locations, themes, and discourses emerged as students addressed and explored their own experiences, subjectivities, and positions. Forging these critical understandings and making them visible to themselves and others allows youth to reflect on their own work and the work of their peers. These visible positionings of youth, in turn, reveal critical understandings in relation to the larger network of social and power relations.

What would happen if teachers and mentors in schools and other formal learning sites were more attentive to the various and shifting affiliations and identity positions of the adolescents they work with? What if the art and media production were more fully integrated into the curriculum? How might we create spaces for adolescents to draw on arts, media, and literacy practices to engage in tactical discursive appropriations and the creation of counter narratives to claim identity positions, to (re)position themselves and others, and to engage them in public dialogue and social critique as part of schooling? What if we put youth claims at the center of our pedagogy? How might we support students as they reach out to a range of public audiences?

Marginalized youth, and/or youth whose academic literacy skills are seen to be inadequate from a schooled perspective or traditional measures, are in fact often flexible creators and designers of multimodal texts and hybrid genres that reflect their subject positions and critical perspectives. New models of authorship, such as those we are arguing for, include sophisticated understandings of the resources of the arts, media, and literacy, and evidence of remixing, mashing, collaging, and assembling of discursive forms (Luke, 2003; Manovich, 2001). What is interesting here for theory and practice in new literacies pedagogy is both the evidence of and potential for creating opportunities for developing discursive sophistication across multimodal intertextuality that cannot be realized through print-dominated pedagogical approaches alone.

Managing these discursive resources requires a sophisticated awareness of the ways in which genre hybridity and multimodal intertextuality are powerful means for the expression of complex cultural ideas, and occasionally reaching toward more emancipatory critical expressions that challenge assumptions about youth, literacy, and society. There are traces of close, engaged reading, as well as wide reading of popular culture and larger societal discourses surrounding the youth in their everyday lives. The ability to engage in textual play, satire, and counter discourses is based on a savvy ability to read into and beyond these cultural texts and to transform them. What similarly innovative and critical reading, writing, and multimodal literacy practices can we find in formal educational settings? If the "voluntary" literacies of these youth are at once artful, playful, and critical, why are school literacies so often lacking in these qualities?

While they have yet to fully find their way to the center of classroom life, these approaches offer new pedagogical spaces within which these expressions might be given close and prioritized attention. These spaces would include both the kinds of critical and textual analysis that has always been central in old literacies, combined with arts and media production—the new media literacies. In such sites, youth would be supported as they negotiate their subject positions and challenge dominant cultural representations and ideologies. There is potential here for both extended peer and larger audiences associated with the fluid nature of arts, media, and new literacy practices to provide a public forum for critical dialogues as well as rich pedagogical sites for further explorations of knowledge production, media representations, and cultural critique.

We acknowledge that these new forms of literacy practice can also serve to obscure or contradict larger purposes of communication. A greater depth of understanding related to conscious control of these tools is as important in new literacies and multiple modalities as in old literacies. For instance, youth arts, media, and critical literacy productions may at times serve to embody, reify, or reinscribe stereotypical or normative cultural discourses and representations as in some productions we describe here and has been observed by other researchers. Pedagogical practices in and out of schools therefore need mentors who can work on these productions alongside youth and participate with them in critical reflection practices. Educators can work within the tensions of a pedagogy in which the self-expressions of youth come into contact with larger discourses as a kind of promise of the democratic citizenship integral to public education.

Our challenge, then, is to transform schools and classrooms to include arts, media, and critical literacy practices that reflect the increasingly multimodal landscapes in which youth reside, rather than limiting themselves to traditional language and literacy discourses and practices. These transformed classrooms would take into account the abilities of students to read, create, perform, film, and integrate knowledge from multiple sources, modes, and forms and to use these resources to engage in social and cultural critique.

How can we build new pedagogies that emanate from practices situated outside of schools—practices that teach and support adolescents as they take up the genres of power and question and critique the ways these literacy practices can serve to include or exclude? We may need new theorizing related to spatiality that allow us to focus on the moments when youth come together to create coherent personal, social, and political messages across educational and community sites. We need to observe how youth draw on virtual and real spaces, and on local and global information and resources to create new forms of cultural participation. Across these spaces, youth are already exhibiting a powerful appropriation of discursive resources and competencies related to cultural analysis and critique that often go unrecognized in today's classrooms.

Educators across a spectrum of "disciplines" can no longer ignore the prevailing integration of arts, media, and literacy produced and consumed in the daily lives and interactions among adolescents. Today's youth engage in complex literacy performances across social and cultural locations. How do we rethink and remake our curricular engagements with adolescents to capture, encourage, and keep up with these sometimes fleeting and powerful literacy practices and cultural productions? How do we engage *with* youth in ways that continue a critical dialogue about the role of these practices at the intersection of education, democracy, and social justice?

Closing Thoughts

To date adolescent critical literacy practices, with their rich fusions of arts and new media in and out of schools, in all of their power, complexity, and reach, remain under-theorized in relation to pedagogy. We envision that this book will extend the conversation about youth literacies by offering a new way to view arts, media, and literacy practices at the intersections of the old and new, local and global, schooled and unschooled, creative and critical. We have provided productive examples of what this new view of literacy practices might look like. At the same time, we acknowledge by working with particular critical themes of homelessness, violence, and discourses of adolescence, and in particular kinds of sites, some approaches, ideas, and products were possible while other important issues were left unexamined.

As this project illustrates, commitments of the youth were sometimes momentary, fragile, and tenuous, and at other times more sustained. Taken together, we found among them an energy and commitment to use critical literacies not only to express who they were and hoped to be, but to engage with the public good, with the democratic project and with larger issues of social justice. We are grateful that they spent time with us, sharing their work and insights; we believe we would do well, as educators, to listen to what they have to say.

References

Alvermann, D. (2002). Effective literacy instruction for adolescents. *Journal of Literacy Research, 34*(2), 189–208.

Anyon, J. (2014). *Radical possibilities: Public policy, urban education and a new social movement* (2nd ed.). New York: Routledge.

Appadurai, A. (1996). *Modernity at large: Cultural dimensions of globalization.* Minneapolis: University of Minneapolis Press.

Bekerman, Z., Burbules, N., & Silberman-Keller, D. (2007). Introduction. In Z. Bekerman, N. Burbules, & D. Silberman-Keller (Eds.), *Learning in places: The informal education reader.* New York: Peter Lang.

Bhabha, H. (1996). Culture's in-between. In S. Hall & P. du Gay (Eds.), *Questions of cultural identity* (pp. 53–60). Thousand Oaks, CA: Sage.

Boler, M. (2008). *Digital media and democracy.* Toronto: University of Toronto Press.

Butler, J. (2009). Performativity, precarity and sexual politics. *Revista de Antropología Iberoamericana, 4*(3), i–xiii.

Dan Rather Reports. (2011). A safe place to shoot up. Retrieved April 12, 2014, from https://www.youtube.com/watch?v=rbxmXja0b9s

Davies, B., & Harre, R. (1990). Positioning: The discursive production of selves. *Journal for the Theory of Social Behaviour, 20*(1), 43–63.

DeCerteau, M. (1984). *The practice of everyday life.* Berkeley: University of California Press.

Dillabough, J., & Kennelly, J. (2010). *Lost youth in the global city: Class, culture and the urban imaginary.* New York: Routledge.

Ellsworth, E. (2005). *Places of learning: Media architecture pedagogy.* New York: RoutledgeFalmer.

Fine, M., Tuck, E., & Yang, K. W. (2014). An intimate memoir of resistance theory. In E. Tuck & K. W. Yang (Eds.), *Youth resistance research and theories of change* (pp. 46–58). New York: Routledge.

Fraser, N. (1990). Rethinking the public sphere: A contribution to the critique of actually existing democracy. *Social Text, 25/26,* 56 80.

Fraser, N. (1993). Rethinking the public sphere: A contribution to the critique of actually existing democracy. In S. During (Ed.), *The cultural studies reader.* pp. 518–536. New York: Routledge.

Giroux, H. (2000). Public pedagogy as cultural politics: Stuart Hall and the "crisis" of culture. *Cultural Studies, 14*(2), 341–360.

Giroux, H. (2005). Cultural studies in dark times: Public pedagogy and the challenge of neoliberalism. *Fast capitalism, 1*(2). Retrieved from http://www.fastcapitalism.com

Grosz, E. (1994). *Volatile bodies: Toward a corporeal feminism.* Bloomington: Indiana University Press.

Grosz, E., & Eisenman, P. (2001). *Architecture from the outside: Essays on virtual and real space.* Cambridge, MA: MIT Press.

Harris, A. (2012). Citizenship stories. In N. Lesko & S. Talburt (Eds.), *Keywords in youth studies: Tracing affects, movements, knowledges* (pp. 143–153). New York: Routledge.

Hickey-Moody, A. (2013). *Youth, arts and education: Reassembling subjectivity through affect.* New York: Routledge.

Holland, D., Lachicotte, W., Skinner, D., & Cain, C. (1998). *Identity and agency in cultural worlds.* Cambridge, MA: Harvard University Press.

Jenkins, H., Clinton, K., Purushotma, R., Robison, A. J., & Weigel, M. (2006). *Confronting the challenges of participatory culture: Media education for the 21st century* (The MacArthur Foundation Report). Retrieved from digitallearning.macfound.org/atf/cf/%7B7E45C7E0-A3E0-4B89-AC9C-E807E1B0AE4E%7D/JENKINS_WHITE_PAPER.PDF

Jocson, K. M. (2013). Remix revisited: Critical solidarity in youth media arts. *E-Learning and Digital Media, 10*(1), 68–82.

Kennelly, J. (2006). "Acting out" in the public sphere. *Canadian Journal of Education, 29*(2), 541–562.

Knobel, M., & Lankshear, C. (2002). Cut, paste, publish: The production and consumption of zines. In D. Alvermann (Ed.), *Adolescents and literacies in a digital world* (pp. 164–185). New York: Peter Lang.

Luke, A., & Elkins, J. (1998). Editorial: Reinventing literacy in "new times." *Journal of Adolescent & Adult Literacy, 42*(1), 4–7.

Luke, C. (2003). Pedagogy, connectivity, multimodality, and interdisciplinarity. *Reading Research Quarterly, 38*(3), 397–403.

Manovich, L. (2001). *The language of new media.* Cambridge, MA: MIT Press.

Massey, D. (2007). *World city.* London: Polity.

Mills, E., & Rogers, T. (Eds.). (2009). *Words from the street: Writings from* Another Slice. Vancouver: SPN Publishing.

New London Group. (1996). A pedagogy of multiliteracies: Designing social futures. *Harvard Educational Review, 66,* 60–92.

Poyntz, S. R. (2008). *Producing publics: An ethnographic study of democratic practice and youth media production and mentorship* (PhD diss.). University of British Columbia, Vancouver. Retrieved from http://hdl.handle.net/2429/2639

Rogers, T. (2000). What will be the social implications and interactions of schooling in the next millenium? *Reading Research Quarterly, 35*(3), 420–421.

Rogers, T., Schroeter, S., Wager, A., & Hauge, C. (2014). Public pedagogies of street-entrenched youth: New literacies, identity and social critique. In K. Sanford, T. Rogers, & M. Kendrick (Eds.), *Everyday youth literacies: Critical perspectives for new times* (pp. 47–61). New York: Springer Publications.

Sandlin, J. A., O'Malley, M. P., & Burdick, J. (2011). Mapping the complexity of public pedagogy scholarship: 1894–2010. *Review of Educational Research, 81*(3), 338–375.

Sandlin, J., Schultz, B. D., & Burdick, J. (Eds.). (2010). *Handbook of public pedagogy.* New York: Routledge.

Soep, E. (2012). Resistance. In N. Lesko & S. Talburt (Eds.), *Keywords in youth studies: Tracing affects, movements, knowledges* (pp. 126–130). New York: Routledge.

Solnit, R., & Schwartzenberg, S. (2000). *Hollow city: The siege of San Francisco and the crisis of American urbanism.* New York: Verso.

Sontag, S. (1999). *Posters, advertisement, art, political artifact, commodity.* In M. Bierut, S. Helfand, S. Heller, & R. Poyner (Eds.), *Looking closer 3: Classic writings on graphic design* (pp. 196–218). New York: Allworth Press.

Talburt, S., & Lesko, N. (2014). Historicizing youth studies. In A. Ibrahim & S. Steinberg (Eds.), *Critical youth studies reader* (pp. 26–37). New York: Peter Lang.

Warner, M. (2002). Publics and counterpublics. *Public Culture, 14*(1), 49–90.

APPENDIX

Descriptions of Arts Pedagogical Practices with Youth

As we stated in the introduction to this book, our general pedagogical approach was to support the youth as they engaged in arts, media, and critical literacy practices. This approach included supporting or actually teaching the youth in a recursive cycle of processes—preparation, inquiry, reflection, and development. While these processes varied across sites, in general we supported youth as they: prepared by generating ideas and developing skills and tools; inquired by unpacking and combining or recombining the material in ways that were suited to the arts or media context; reflected through sharing and discussing initial products and performances; and developed their projects through further reflection and reframing, and moved toward sharing with audiences. We provided this support as needed and requested; the youth more independently produced writings, art, media, and performances.

All of the practices described below require varying kinds of physical space and materials for writing, rehearsing, performing, filming, editing, and publishing.

Illustration of Zine Practices with Youth

Zines are noncommercial publications in which authors represent their identities, stories, and culture. The zine provided a pedagogical space in which modes, media resources, and critical reflections collided. Drawing on the youth's personal experiences as well as themes that related to their lives (e.g., tattoos, social workers), the youth at this site unpacked and remixed material in order to gather together and build community, to create art, engage in civic action, and to speak back to the ways they were positioned by society.

Preparation

The youth we worked with were highly transient, often traveling across the country one or more times in a year. Attendance varied from two or three to twenty youth at any given meeting. They may not have seen each other for weeks or even months, especially in the autumn as many of them began to return to Vancouver for the winter months. Thus, in order to reconnect, collaborate, and brainstorm ideas for their creative projects, they appreciated the structured together time offered by the Sunday evening zine meetings (a place, a set timeframe, food). However, within this structured time, it was important to use a flexible approach, as the street youth were wary of any "top-down" school-like practices.

At the beginning of each *Another Slice* zine session, the youth gathered around a meal in order to reconnect with one another and to discuss what had been happening in their lives over the past weeks/months. Guidelines for the meetings were laid out by a youth leader or staff facilitator and included showing respect, not talking while others were talking, and so forth. Announcements were also made regarding relevant events, upcoming zine themes, the status of the zine they were currently working on, and pending deadlines.

Examples of Preparation during Meetings

At most meetings, as the youth arrived, each took a slice of pizza and some pop that had been provided for them. They put their heavy backpacks down and participated in a youth-led group discussion. For instance, a participant might talk about how the group might gain access to free condoms or clean needles. Others may react, perhaps mentioning local outreach programs, including their interests in protecting each other and/or cleaning up the city.

On one evening, the youth were discussing their various living arrangements. One young man talked about how he wanted to get a place in a nearby city because he was tired of having his possessions stolen from him while in a shelter. He discussed the potential of moving in with a foster parent. On other evenings the youth talked about and shared their tattoos, or other topics of interest.

At some point (depending on the length of the informal conversation) more formal announcements were made. The youth leader or staff facilitator would typically state the guidelines, share any additional announcements, and explain what was happening that evening (including occasional workshops led by local artists).

Inquiry

Inquiry in zine making often stemmed from discussions as described above. Youth worked creatively in isolation or with others to work on projects, which may or may not eventually be included in the zine.

Examples of the Inquiry Process

On the same evening the young man who wanted to get a place in a nearby city decided to write an essay about the housing situations of various street-entrenched youth. On another evening, a youth shared a new tattoo that he received. Following a discussion on where to go to get the best tattoo, others shared their tattoos and the stories that surrounded them. When the idea came up to devote an issue to tattoos, the youth began to design drawings of a new tattoo or of the equipment needed to tattoo someone. Others decided they might take photos of their tattoos. These inquires might, at times, be taking place during boisterous discussions or debates, and at other times in silence, depending on the form and topic being explored.

As researchers we noticed that the street youth enjoyed activities that were portable (e.g., writing poems, creating small art projects, reading paperback books) or wearable (e.g., clothing, tattoos). Some of their inquiries led to projects outside of the zine. For instance, at one meeting a young woman explained that she enjoyed sewing as a hobby. She then showed us her newly designed bra. She had demonstrated creativity by sewing black leather straps onto it and including front clasps. It also had red stitching. Her exploration and demonstration led to questions from the group, as well as the creation of undergarments for other street youth.

Another participant brought up the idea of quillos—a combination of pillow and quilt, complete with a stash pocket. These items were relevant to the other youth because they were portable and because they would keep them warm during the colder nights. Jae and a youth worker talked about their interests in sewing and owning a business. They expressed a desire to create a quillo prototype in order to approach the Hudson's Bay Company. If their idea took off, it was their intent to give one quillo to Directions and one to Common House (a local shelter) for each quillo sold.

Reflection

Reflection happened throughout each zine meeting. At times reflections took the forms of written poems, interviews, and active discussions, and at other times youth reflected through drawing pictures or by taking photographs. Some reflections inspired zine themes, as in the example above that led to an issue focused on tattoos. At another time during the year, after the participants were reflecting on the lack of community resources and support provided for street-entrenched youth, the participants decided to create a zine for social workers, advising them how to handle particular situations.

Example of Facilitating a Reflection

As researchers, we noticed that some of the best poetry arose out of the participants' situated conversations and understandings. For example, after a visiting arts facilitator led a long (one and one half hour), highly structured poetry workshop we recognized that the youth felt resistant and disengaged, calling it a shitty Sunday. In order to re-engage them, Theresa asked the youth to reflect upon their ideas regarding "Shitty Sundays," noting what they felt like, tasted like, and smelled like to create a group poem. The youth seemed to enjoy the collaborative process of creating a collective poem out of their own conversation. Later one of the youth (Tweek) said that he viewed the reflection as "a relief," because it provided a way for him "to get the crap out of his head."

At other times the reflection process included supporting the youth as they collected various art projects, writings, and photographs and moved toward creating a zine. For the social worker zine, we worked with a youth who had a lot to say about the assumptions social workers made about street youth but resisted writing his thoughts down. We suggested that we turn his thoughts into an interview that could be transcribed and included, which he and a friend agreed to.

Development

Developing counter narratives that interrupt or reject the ways that society positions homeless youth became a goal or outcome for many of the participants involved. These claims were developed and disseminated inside and outside of our research sessions, taking multiple forms including: essays, interviews, drawings, paintings, films, and poems. The youth were interested in voicing their opinions (going public, so to speak), while at the same time creating a stronger local community.

Examples of the Development Process

An example of the development process is described in the opening vignette of Chapter 2 in which Kari-Lynn helped Jordan to create a poem to express his concerns about rigs (used needles) being dropped near playgrounds and parks. While Jordan initially struggled to express his ideas, when Kari-Lynn suggested the concrete poetry form she helped him to frame his ideas in a way that could be effectively shared. The result was an assemblage of modes (Winters, 2010), eventually becoming a multimodal poster-like page in an unthemed issue of the zine.

On another evening we suggested to the youth that they could pull their best poetry from the zine and include new poetry to create a chapbook anthology, explaining what a chapbook was and how the selection might be curated, and how we might move toward publication. The youth worker who oversaw the zine program at that time was also very interested in supporting this process. As we noted, the chapbook, *Words from the Street* (Mills and Rogers, 2009), was eventually published. Local community workers, scholars, facilitators, and youth were formally invited to the Gathering Place, a local space where youth felt welcomed and included, for a book launch. The poems were shared using an open mic format. One youth, Fraggle, shared her poem called "The Truth (hurts)" (Rawk, 2009).

This public forum gave Fraggle the opportunity to speak back to the ways in which she was being marginalized within public spaces, and at the same time to ask questions: ". . . if it all were to come crashing down, who will be the one left shivering in the cold?"(p. 11.)

Illustration of Filmic Practices with Youth

The filmmaking processes in this project provided pedagogical spaces for the youth to combine and recombine written, spoken, visual, and aural forms and modes, including narrative, interviews, photography, video, and music, and to playfully and seriously address issues of violence in their lives and communities.

Preparation

In the *preparation* phase of development, there is a need for plentiful viewing of images and film clips. The viewing serves two purposes—the first as a catalyst for discussion and the second as a naturally occurring visual and auditory means to plan. Projecting a story in one's mind in preparation for filming or editing requires a vocabulary of imagery. Viewing, like reading print, helps to point out the "grammar and syntax" of filmic works (LaMonde, 2011) to establish some parameters, but also to open the space for reconceptualization or remixing. In Chapter 3, we offer several examples of instances when youth were first invited to view a clip from a film, which was either intended to illustrate a filmic style or spark ideas. The youth, therefore, often screened peer-constructed short films, university student short films, and clips of professional films (such as *Reel Bad Arabs*). All such viewings led to rich discussions and frequently sparked a vision for creating a short film. At other times the viewing facilitated a model that prepared the means for creating their own ideas not yet storyboarded.

Inquiry

The *inquiry* phase of film production involves conceptualizing, dialoguing, and data gathering. Viewing other films sparks inquiry—everything from the medium, i.e., how something was filmed and edited (the filmmaker's vision), to the message the film is intending to convey. Every stage of inquiry is a step toward representing critical thinking and capturing the creative spark. In film production, as with other collaborative literacy forms, there is a need for inquiry teams as there is a need for production teams. Dialogue is a key to this process and often launches into scouting for tangibles, e.g., searching the Internet for images and music playlists to be used, or finding the right location and setting up the perfect film shot. There were many instances of inquiry illustrated in the book; one example, however, that stands out is Kaity's diligent investigation into the personality, social context, and existential parallels of Billie Holiday (see Chapter 3). Another, *Teenage Kicks*, in which the parody involved many participants both on and off camera, motivated an inquiry into the qualities and boundaries for creating a satire and its eventual reception. The latter included inquiry into audience reception, or imagining how others may perceive the message.

Reflection

Reflection during the filmmaking process emerges at several stages. During the critical decision making stage, much reflection is done "on the spot" while reviewing images and sound in playback. This ongoing reflective mode is similar to the kind of revisions and editing processes in which a good writer typically engages. From storyboarding to final edit, film teams preview the potential images and storied text, decide on or adapt the film's genre or forms (e.g., a documentary, a parody, an interview, a fictional narrative), and construct the final edit in post-production. With each stage of development, a reflection on the part is made to fit the whole. Whether filming a "trial" run and then critiquing it in playback, or deciding on post-production inserts (e.g., to make something more explicit or to deepen the message by widening its meaning), the youth as filmmakers were engaged in reflective dialogue with each other.

Of course, the final edit of a film invites a richer and more complex reflection from each individual. At that final production stage, all filmmakers reflect on the serendipitous and creative impulses, inspirational moments that shifted the narrative, or the manner through which the unconscious past filters into their expression. It was no different for youth filmmakers. The final films became either a talking point for extending thoughts or a reflection on the making of the film. At each public screening, the youth, as filmmakers, discussed and reflected on their films—in particular with respect to audience reception—in sophisticated and critical ways.

Development

The *development* phase of filmmaking, that is the extension, enriching, or otherwise deepening of the conceptual framework or a story idea, is found in post-production. During the editing of a final version, the filmmaker must make a decision as to whether to match intended goals, which were planned at the outset, with captured footage, or to take the ideas into a new direction by adding or deleting footage, including written text (titles and inter-titles), additional dialogue (e.g., voice-over narratives) and special effects. The new direction often occurs when a "hidden meaning" is made more explicit to the filmmakers through the imagery. One example of this type of development is illustrated in one of the *24 Frames per Second* shorts. Although the shorts began as a series of shots woven together in the style of Chris Marker's *La Jetée* to create a "still frame" narrative, they each progressed through added footage, i.e., filming live, and a post-interview voice-over. In one such film, the concept was finalized out of the serendipitous, as is often the case in filmmaking, and simply followed a natural progression of creating a story through filmic texts by adding the meaningful and deleting the superfluous.

Illustration of Performance Practices with Youth

Performance practices include participants (and facilitators), adequate spaces for warming up, time for rehearsing and performing, and a range of materials, including texts, images, sounds, lighting, props, and costumes. Devising practices allow for rich possibilities of creation, embodied performance, and the combination of media and modalities to express ideas, experiences, and imaginings that originate with participants' own interests and lives.

Preparation

Some sort of "warm-up" or introductory exercise is crucial to the majority of performance-based inquiry and performance creation. In order for the work to be exploratory, rich, and creative, participants need to be comfortable, or at least feel connected with their physical bodies; they need to be aware of the space and other participants in the space; they need to feel safe; they need to be focused and mentally present. These are significant demands at the best of times, but especially so in the context of the typical school setting. There are myriad ways to warm up a group; below is one example that was used in this project.

Example of a Preparation/Warm-up Strategy: "Walking a Web"

Stand in a circle. One person says his or her name and then "to" the name of someone else in the circle, e.g., "Jamie to Danny." Having said that, the person speaking (in this case, Jamie) begins to walk through the circle to the person whose name they spoke and stands in their place in the circle (in this case, Danny). At the same time, the person whose name has been beckoned (Danny) repeats the process, i.e. "Danny to Drew." Danny immediately moves to Drew's space, allowing Jamie to step into his/her space. And the exchanges continue in this way until everyone has walked through the circle at least once.

Inquiry

Inquiry during performance work typically involves moving across mediums and modalities in order to explore expression and representation in different forms. Through the pursuit of representation, participants engage in exploration of the initial idea (think of Marjorie Siegel's (1995) concept of transmediation, and/or Richardson and St. Pierre's (2005) concepts of writing as inquiry). Inquiry can take place using image theatre, such as embodying ideas in tableaux (for more on image theatre see for example Boal, 1979, 1995, 2002); it could involve improvised dialogue or movement (for more on improvisation see for example Johnstone, 1987; Jones and Kelly, 2007); it could involve creating soundscapes (from voices, found objects, musical instruments, and composition); or it could involve visual composition, using digital imagery for example, or a combination of bodies positioned in relation to space and images. Below is an example of inquiry through improvisation.

An Example of Facilitating an Inquiry Using Structured Improvisation

The process begins with establishing the topic, object, text, etc. to be explored. The next step is to decide who is to take part (the whole group, or certain individuals) and give some time to think about or discuss the context within which participants will enter the improvised scene. Next, a decision is made regarding whether the improvisation will take place in the foreground or background, as well as whether music or recorded sound will be used, or if it is to take place in silence, and whether spoken words are encouraged or discouraged. Ground rules are established, if required. For example, a recognizable signal to begin the improvisation (e.g., "begin," "take it away," a clap of hands) and a signal to end the scene is provided. At Lismore, a class discussion took place leading to the proposal by a student of an idea for performance. The student described her idea as a scene in which people are coming and going through the performance space, each carrying some sort of bag, container, or luggage. The other students discussed it, and Mia proceeded to set up an improvisation based on it. Each student found a bag of some kind, music was selected, and a projector screen was set up at the back of the space to allow students to play with shadows and silhouettes. The improvisation lasted approximately ten minutes, during which time all students explored entering and exiting the space, relating to other performances and to their bags. Finally, in a group discussion after the improvisation, reflection, impressions, and ideas are shared. This improvisation proved to explore characters, themes, as well as transitional choreography for the final performance (see Chapter 4).

Reflection

Reflection in performance work bears resemblance to spectatorship (of self and peers). It is an integral time in which to share, as a group, ideas and responses about the presentation, the space, individual relationships to ideas being explored, and emerging interests. It should be a space where participants can consolidate ideas and come together on shared interests, but also a space in which participants can maintain conflicting views, can debate diverse perspectives, and ultimately continue inquiry through discussion.

Example of Facilitating a Reflection

Depending on the nature of the group and the experience of the facilitator, reflections can be organic and open ended—an open forum within which participants can assert ideas, pose questions, brainstorm, and debate. In other circumstances, a format for discussion can be facilitated that controls the process more predictably. One such format is the Critical Response Process (see Lerman, 2003). This method involves four main steps:

1. Statements of Meaning: Responders state what was meaningful, evocative, interesting, exciting, or striking in the work they have just witnessed.
2. Artist as Questioner: The artist asks questions about the work. After each question, the responders answer. Responders may express opinions if they are in direct response to the question asked and do not contain suggestions for changes.
3. Neutral Questions: Responders ask neutral questions about the work. The artist responds. Questions are neutral when they do not have an opinion couched in them. For example, if you are discussing the lighting of a scene, "Why was it so dark?" is not a neutral question. "What ideas guided your choices about lighting?" is.
4. Opinion Time: Responders state opinions, subject to permission from the artist. The usual form is "I have an opinion about _____, would you like to hear it?" The artist has the option to say no.

In improvisations in which the whole class or group is involved, a more organic facilitation may be preferred. For instance, in the above-mentioned improvisation, a number of students focused their reflections on the modality shift at work in the improvisation (which occurred to the background of music, and required no specific verbal text). Sam, for example, "liked how . . . you could just go up to someone else's character and just have a conversation without even saying anything, you could just like with eye contact or something . . ." Kyle adds: "Because we couldn't talk that much . . . we had to express ourselves with our movement and our facial expressions, so while we were still our characters we were almost overdoing them so that we could get our point across whenever we interacted with someone else." Victoria refers to the character inquiry involved in the improvisation: "It helped because I know a little bit about my character but not everything . . . thinking about how is my character going up to other people because you wouldn't necessarily know that . . . so it helped build my character."

Development

In performance work, development depends on the objectives at hand. Assuming the process engaged in has a goal of performance creation, the development steps of the work include the reviewing of ideas, texts (broadly defined), scenes, characters, and so on, that have been explored, and selecting directions for ongoing work. The work required will be completely dependent on the results of the inquiry in relation to the object and objectives of the inquiry.

Examples of Development Work

Groupings of participants to work on specific aspects of the performance, finalizing and scripting a scene (likely to involve writing the text chosen from improvised iterations of a scene), researching a topic, an era, or a person; creating a slide show or digital media element for the performance, developing a monologue, choreographing a movement sequence, etc. For the development process of the final performance at Lismore Secondary (see Chapter 4), processes included selecting and ordering scenes to be included, editing and finalizing scripts, rehearsing scenes, creating a visual slideshow to project into the space, deciding on a name for the performance, and the list goes on.

References

Boal, A. (1979). *Theatre of the oppressed* (Trans. C. A. McBride & M.O.L. McBride). New York: Theatre Communications Group.
Boal, A. (1995). *The rainbow of desire* (Trans. A. Jackson). New York: Routledge.
Boal, A. (2002). *Games for actors and non-actors* (Trans. A. Jackson). New York: Routledge.
Johnstone, K. (1987). *Impro: Improvisation and the theatre.* New York: Routledge.
Jones, J., & Kelly, M. (2007). *Drama games and improvs.* Colorado Springs, CO: Meriwether Publishing.
LaMonde, A. M. (2011). *The neuroscience of movement, time and space: An arts educational study of the embodied brain* (PhD diss.). University of British Columbia, Vancouver. Retrieved from https://circle.ubc.ca/handle/2429/33961?show=full
Lerman, L. (2003). Retrieved from http://danceexchange.org/projects/critical-response-process
Mills, E. and Rogers, T. (Eds). *Words from the street: Writings from* Another Slice. Vancouver: SPN Publishing.
Rawk, F. (2009). The Truth (hurts). In E. Mills & T. Rogers (Eds.), *Words from the street: Writings from* Another Slice. pp. 10–11. Vancouver: SPN Publishing.
Richardson, L., & St. Pierre, E. (2005). Writing: A method of inquiry. In N.K. Denzin & Y.S. Lincoln (Eds.), *Handbook of qualitative research* (3rd ed., pp. 959–978). Thousand Oaks, CA: Sage.
Siegel, M. (1995). More than words: The generative power of transmediation for learning. *Canadian Journal of Education, 20*(4), 455–475.
Winters, K. (2010). Quilts of authorship: A literature review of multimodal assemblage in the field of literacy education. *Canadian Journal for New Scholars in Education, 3*(1), 1–12.

INDEX

CPSIA information can be obtained
at www.ICGtesting.com
Printed in the USA
BVHW04s0417080818
R8909700001B/R89097PG523237BVX2B/2/P

9 781138 017450